CHINESE
cooking & more

pil

Publications International, Ltd.

Pictured on the front cover *(clockwise from top left):* Thai Seitan Stir-Fry *(page 142),* Thai Salad Rolls with Spicy Sweet & Sour Sauce *(page 22),* Asian Honey-Tea Grilled Prawns *(page 200)* and Spicy Fried Rice with Tofu *(page 148).*
Pictured on the back cover *(counterclockwise from top):* Shrimp, Mushroom and Omelet Soup *(page 64),* Baked Egg Rolls *(page 206)* and Soba Stir-Fry *(page 82).*

ISBN-13: 978-1-4508-7324-6
ISBN-10: 1-4508-7324-3

Library of Congress Control Number: 2012934847

Manufactured in China.

8 7 6 5 4 3 2 1

Microwave Cooking: Microwave ovens vary in wattage. Use the cooking times as guidelines and check for doneness before adding more time.

Preparation/Cooking Times: Preparation times are based on the approximate amount of time required to assemble the recipe before cooking, baking, chilling or serving. These times include preparation steps such as measuring, chopping and mixing. The fact that some preparations and cooking can be done simultaneously is taken into account. Preparation of optional ingredients and serving suggestions is not included.

Publications International, Ltd.

Table of Contents

Asian Cooking for American Kitchens

It's not surprising that Asian food is an American favorite. We may have started with chop suey brought home in a little paper carton with a handle, but we've graduated to an appreciation of everything from sushi and Thai curry to authentic Szechuan cuisine and Korean tacos.

Asian food fits with the way we eat now. It uses a little bit of meat or fish to add savor to a large amount of vegetables and rice. It celebrates the freshness of vegetables and the rich, umami flavor of mushrooms and soy sauce. Creating the distinctive flavors and contrasting textures of Asian cuisine in a home kitchen is less difficult than you would think. The recipes in this book use techniques and ingredients that will be mostly familiar to you. A few less mainstream products, like miso, dried shiitakes or curry paste can usually be found in the Asian aisle of the supermarket, purchased online or found at a specialty store.

Stir-Fry Savvy

Many Asian recipes are stir-fried. Organization is the key to success. There are often numerous ingredients that need to be cut into bite-size pieces before you start cooking. It's best to have small bowls lined up next to the stove holding individual ingredients so you won't waste time searching for something at the last minute.

You don't have to have a wok to stir-fry, but it just may be the most versatile cooking vessel ever invented. You can stir-fry, sauté, braise or deep-fry in a wok. It can also serve as a skillet, a soup pot or a steamer. There are many kinds of woks available, but an inexpensive carbon steel model, seasoned according to the manufacturer's instructions, works well. Beware of some nonstick-coated pans and electric woks. They can't get hot enough safely to handle real stir-fying. You can easily use a large deep skillet instead of a wok. Make sure that it can withstand high heat and that it is heavy enough to retain it. Rounded sides will make it easier to toss ingredients or remove them as needed.

Rice 101

Most Asian meals include rice in some form. And, as a visit to any Asian market will prove, it comes in many forms and varieties. The two most basic types are long grain and short grain. Long grain rice has slender grains that cook up relatively firm and fluffy. Short grain rice, which can be almost round, has an outer layer that absorbs

4

water easily, so the cooked product is soft and a bit sticky. This is an advantage when you want to roll it into sushi or pick it up with chopsticks. Sushi rice and arborio rice are short grain. Jasmine and basmati are examples of long grain varieties. Brown rice is any variety that has not been polished to remove the rice bran layer and the germ. It retains vitamins and fiber, but takes considerably longer to cook and is more perishable. White rice is preferred in Asian cuisines.

Asian Noodles

Thick or thin, curly or flat, made of wheat, rice and even buckwheat, Asian noodles offer a continent's worth of flavors and textures to explore. Next time you want to turn vegetables into a meal, just start noodling around.

Chinese wheat noodles (mein) are similar to pasta and come in just as many styles and shapes with or without the addition of egg. They are cooked like pasta, so you can substitute a similar pasta shape if you have trouble finding the Asian version.

Secrets to Perfect Rice

1. Use Very Low Heat. If you don't have a burner that holds a low simmer, invest in a device called a heat diffuser or "flame tamer." This round, perforated metal disc rests right on the burner, under the saucepan, to keep the heat even.

2. Don't Peek! Once the saucepan is covered, don't open it until the cooking time is up. Even a small loss of heat can make a real difference.

3. Invest in a Rice Cooker. Most Asian cooks use one. Rice cookers not only turn out perfect rice every time, most will keep it warm for you, too.

Rice noodles come in a dizzying array of sizes and go by a confusing number of names—rice sticks and rice vermicelli are two. Southeast Asian cooking uses rice noodles for many classic dishes including Pad Thai (recipe on page 98). Unlike wheat noodles, rice noodles only need to be soaked in hot water before using.

Soba noodles are flat Japanese noodles made with buckwheat flour, which gives them an earthy, nutty flavor. They are served cold during Japanese summers and hot in winter soups. Soba should be cooked until tender, not al dente.

Udon noodles are thick, white Japanese or Korean noodles made from wheat flour and water. They are typically served in broth.

basil: Several varieties of basil are used in Asian cooking, including Thai basil, which has an anise-mint flavor and purple stems, and holy basil, which has a sharp, spicy-hot taste. Ordinary sweet basil is quite close in flavor to Thai basil and is a readily available substitute.

bean sprouts: The crisp, delicate sprouts of mung beans are extremely perishable. Purchase bean sprouts that have their buds attached and that smell and look fresh, not musty or slimy. Refrigerate sprouts and use within a few days.

black bean sauce/hot black bean sauce: Bean sauces are made from fermented black soybeans (sometimes called salted or dried black beans). Additional flavorings may include garlic, sugar and rice wine and, in the case of hot black bean sauce, chile peppers.

bok choy: The name bok choy means white vegetable and is a catch-all term for the many related Asian cabbages. Here the most common is the bok choy with green leaves and thick white stems. You will also find a smaller version labeled baby bok choy. The choy with green stems is often referred to as Shanghai choy. Almost all varieties are interchangeable and have similar flavors.

chile peppers: Both fresh and dried chile peppers are used. There are hundreds of varieties of fresh chiles. Jalapeño or serrano peppers are readily available and work well in Asian dishes. Dried red chile peppers are even hotter than fresh ones and can be slightly tamed by removing the seeds. In many recipes in this book, dried red pepper flakes are called for instead of whole chiles as they are easier to find. Fresh or dried, care should be taken when handling chile peppers since they can sting and irritate the skin. Wear gloves when handling peppers and do not touch your eyes. Be sure to wash your hands and all surfaces and utensils that have been in contact with the peppers after handling.

coconut milk: Unsweetened canned coconut milk is available in the ethnic sections of most supermarkets. Do not confuse it with cream of coconut which is a sweetened product used in drinks like piña coladas. Nor is coconut milk the liquid inside a fresh coconut (that's coconut water). Coconut milk is made by combining water and the meat from a coconut, simmering and straining out solids.

chili garlic sauce or paste: This fiery combination of crushed red chiles and puréed garlic is available in many varieties and brands. The paste is more concentrated, so if you are substituting, use less.

curry pastes and powders: Most well-stocked supermarkets carry Thai red and green curry pastes in the Asian section. They can also be ordered online. They are made of chile peppers, lemongrass, shallots, garlic, ginger, coriander and cumin. Unless you're familiar with the product, always start by adding less curry paste than the recipe directs, since heat levels vary considerably from brand to brand. Curry powder comes in a variety of formulations as well. Indian curry powder is a mixture of as many as 20 different spices including chiles, cinnamon, cumin, fennel seeds, ginger, coriander and turmeric. Chinese and Southeast Asian curries may use their own different blends, but Madras curry powder is a good mainstream choice for all South Asian curries.

dashi: Used in miso soup and many other Japanese recipes, dashi is a stock or broth made with dried bonito (tuna) flakes and kelp.

five-spice powder: A mixture of ground cinnamon, cloves, fennel seeds, star anise and Szechuan peppercorns, five-spice powder is part of many Chinese dishes. It is said to include all five flavors—sweet, sour, salty, bitter and pungent.

fish sauce: This condiment is used in Southeast Asian cooking as soy sauce is in Chinese cuisine. Don't be put off by its funky aroma, which diminishes with cooking. Fish sauce helps balance and complete many dishes. It is possible to substitute soy sauce, but the results will be different.

ginger, fresh: Fresh ginger is the rhizome (an underground stem) of the ginger plant. It's a knobby, bumpy, beige root that you will find in the produce section. Ground ginger comes from the same plant, but has a different flavor.

ginger, pickled: These thin slices of fresh ginger are preserved in a vinegar pickling solution and served with sushi or used as a garnish in Japanese cuisine.

hoisin sauce: This thick reddish-brown sauce is sweet, salty and a bit spicy. It contains soybeans, chile peppers and various spices and is used in Peking duck along with other classic barbecue dishes.

lemongrass: The flowery perfume of lemongrass is one of the most delightful elements of Thai cooking. Minced finely, lemongrass is part of many curry pastes. The stalks are also cut into large pieces and used to flavor foods, rather like a bay leaf, then removed before serving. To use fresh lemongrass, cut off the moist portion at the root end. Throw away the dry, fibrous stalk and the outer leaves. The tender white portion may then be minced and used. Lemongrass freezes well. Grated lemon peel may be substituted, but with a substantial difference in flavor.

mirin: Mirin is a very sweet golden wine used in many Japanese sauces, marinades and glazes. It is not usually consumed as a beverage.

miso: This fermented, soy-based seasoning paste has a smooth, buttery texture and a tangy, salty taste. Japanese miso soup (recipe on page 78) is the most common use, but miso is also used in dressings, marinades and sauces.

nori: These paper-thin sheets of seaweed are dry and dark greenish-black. Most nori is used to wrap sushi and is pre-toasted (yaki-nori). It can also be crumbled over rice or added to salads.

oyster sauce: A rich-tasting, dark brown sauce made from oysters, soy sauce and often MSG. Check the label to see if the sauce you're purchasing contains real oyster extract or just oyster flavoring.

rice noodles: These semi-translucent dried noodles come in many sizes and have many names, including rice stick noodles, rice-flour noodles and pho noodles. Widths range from string thin (usually called rice vermicelli) to 1 inch wide. All rice noodles must be soaked or boiled before using and all may be used interchangeably provided soaking and cooking times are adjusted.

rice papers: Look for packages containing stacks of thin translucent rounds, 6 to 8 inches in diameter, in Asian markets. Rice papers look incredibly fragile but are actually fairly easy to handle. After soaking they become soft, flexible and a bit stretchy.

rice vinegar: Both Chinese and Japanese rice vinegars are made from fermented glutinous (sweet) rice. They are milder than regular white vinegars and also have a bit of sweetness. Seasoned rice vinegar has salt and sugar added and is used to flavor sushi rice.

rice wine: This slightly sweet wine is made from fermented glutinous rice. Shaoxing rice wine is a good variety. Avoid those labeled "cooking wine," since they often have salt or sugar added.

shiitake mushrooms: Shiitakes can be purchased fresh or dried. The dried ones are often simply called Chinese black mushrooms. The meaty texture and flavor of shiitakes works well in many preparations. The stems of shiitakes are woody and tough. Discard them or save them for flavoring soup or stock.

soy sauce: The quality of soy sauce can vary greatly. It is made from soybeans and roasted grain (usually wheat). Look for sauce that is naturally brewed. Cheaper soy sauce is often manufactured from hydrolyzed vegetable protein with corn syrup and color added. Regular soy sauce is sometimes referred to as light soy sauce and is the commonly available variety (not to be confused with reduced-sodium or "lite" soy). Dark soy sauce is brewed longer and is thicker and sweeter.

sushi rice: Rice prepared for sushi is the short-grain variety. It is boiled, then quickly cooled and dressed with seasoned rice vinegar. If you can't find a produce labeled "sushi rice", use another short-grain white rice.

straw mushrooms: Traditionally grown on straw used in rice paddies, straw mushrooms are available in cans in Asian markets. They are sometimes labeled "peeled" or "unpeeled," which refers to whether or not the caps have opened. Rinse carefully and drain straw mushrooms before using them.

Szechuan pepper/peppercorns: This mildly hot spice is no relation to black peppercorns or chile peppers. It has a slightly flowery, lemony flavor and aroma and a unique tongue-numbing effect. Szechuan peppercorns are sometimes available in powdered form, but whole peppercorns are most often crushed right before using to release their flavor.

9

tamari: A Japanese version of soy sauce, tamari has a slightly thicker consistency and a stronger but mellower flavor. It is brewed like soy sauce, but usually does not contain wheat, which is an advantage for those who are sensitive to gluten.

tofu: Versatile tofu, also called bean curd, is a custard-like cake pressed from cooked ground soybeans. You can purchase it in soft, firm or extra-firm styles. Bland by itself, tofu readily takes on the flavors of whatever it is cooked with. It is low in calories, high in protein and cholesterol free.

wasabi: This bright green condiment is sold in the form of a powder, which must be reconstituted with water, or a paste. It's known as Japanese horseradish because it has the same powerful, sinus-clearing flavor.

wonton wrappers: Sometimes called wonton skins, these extremely thin sheets of dough are made of flour and water. In supermarkets, they are usually found in the refrigerated section near tofu. A 12-ounce package contains 4 or 5 dozen wrappers.

Dumplings & Wraps

Every Asian cuisine offers a mouthwatering array of flavorful bite-size treats. Whether you prefer Chinese pot stickers, Japanese gyoza or Vietnamese Summer Rolls, these recipes prove that delicious things come in small packages.

chicken gyoza

¼ pound ground chicken
¼ cup finely chopped napa cabbage
1 green onion, minced
1½ teaspoons soy sauce
½ teaspoon minced fresh ginger
½ teaspoon cornstarch
22 gyoza or pot sticker wrappers
2 tablespoons vegetable oil
Dipping Sauce (recipe follows)

1. Combine chicken, cabbage, green onion, soy sauce, ginger and cornstarch in medium bowl; stir well.

2. Place 1 rounded teaspoonful chicken filling in center of gyoza wrapper. Dampen edges of wrapper with wet finger. Pull sides of wrapper together; press to seal. Pleat edges of gyoza by making small folds. Place on lightly oiled surface while filling remaining gyoza.

3. Heat oil in large skillet over medium heat. Add 8 to 10 gyoza to skillet; do not crowd. Cook 3 minutes per side or until golden brown and filling is cooked through. Keep warm while frying remaining gyoza. Serve with Dipping Sauce.

Makes 22 gyoza

Dipping Sauce: Combine ¼ cup soy sauce, 2 teaspoons mirin (Japanese sweet rice wine) and ¼ to ½ teaspoon chili oil in small bowl. Stir well.

vietnamese summer rolls

Vietnamese Dipping Sauce (recipe follows)
½ pound medium raw shrimp, peeled and deveined
3½ ounces thin rice noodles (rice vermicelli)
12 rice paper wrappers,* about 6 inches in diameter
36 whole fresh cilantro leaves
¼ pound roast pork or beef, sliced ⅛ inch thick
1 tablespoon chopped peanuts
Lime peel (optional)

Rice paper is a thin, edible wrapper used in Southeast Asian cooking.

1. Prepare Vietnamese Dipping Sauce; set aside.

2. Bring large saucepan of water to a boil over high heat. Add shrimp; simmer 1 to 2 minutes or until pink and opaque. Remove shrimp with slotted spoon to small bowl. When cool, slice shrimp in half lengthwise.

3. Meanwhile, soften rice noodles in medium bowl of hot water 20 to 30 minutes or according to package directions. Drain; cut noodles into 3-inch lengths.

4. Soften rice paper wrappers in large bowl of warm water 30 to 40 seconds or until pliable. Drain wrappers, one at a time, on paper towels and transfer to work surface. Arrange three cilantro leaves in center of wrapper. Layer with two shrimp halves, pork and rice noodles.

5. Fold bottom of wrapper up over filling; fold in each side and roll up to enclose filling. Repeat with remaining wrappers and filling.

6. Sprinkle with peanuts just before serving. Garnish with lime peel. Serve with Vietnamese Dipping Sauce.   *Makes 12 summer rolls*

Vietnamese Dipping Sauce: Combine ½ cup water, ¼ cup fish sauce, 2 tablespoons lime juice, 1 tablespoon sugar, 1 clove minced garlic and ¼ teaspoon chili oil in small bowl; mix well. Makes about 1 cup.

crab rangoon with spicy dipping sauce

Dipping Sauce

1 cup ketchup
¼ cup chili garlic sauce
4 teaspoons Chinese hot mustard

Crab Rangoon

1 package (8 ounces) cream cheese, softened
1 can (6 ounces) lump crabmeat, well drained*
⅓ cup minced green onions
1 package wonton wrappers
1 egg white, beaten
Vegetable oil for frying

*Pick out and discard any shell or cartilage from crabmeat.

1. Combine ketchup, chili garlic sauce and mustard in small bowl; set aside.

2. Beat cream cheese in medium bowl until light and fluffy. Stir in crabmeat and green onions.

3. Place wrapper on work surface. Place 1 rounded teaspoon crab mixture in center. Brush edges of wrapper with egg white. Fold diagonally in half (wonton wrappers are not quite square so they will not form perfect triangles); press edges firmly to seal. Repeat with remaining wrappers and filling.

4. Heat 2 inches oil in Dutch oven to 350°F. Add wontons, a few at a time; do not crowd. Fry on one side 2 minutes or until golden; turn and fry 2 minutes or until second side is golden. Remove with slotted spoon and drain on paper towels. Serve immediately with Dipping Sauce.   *Makes about 44 wontons*

Variation: Crab Rangoon can be baked instead of fried, but the results will not be as crisp or as golden in color. Prepare as directed through Step 3, then arrange triangles 1 inch apart on parchment-lined baking sheets. Spray tops of triangles with nonstick cooking spray. Bake in preheated 375°F oven about 11 minutes or until lightly browned. Serve immediately.

thai lamb & couscous rolls

5 cups water, divided
16 large napa cabbage leaves, stems trimmed
2 tablespoons minced fresh ginger
1 teaspoon red pepper flakes
⅔ cup uncooked couscous
½ pound lean ground lamb
½ cup chopped green onions
3 cloves garlic, minced
¼ cup plus 2 tablespoons minced fresh cilantro or mint, divided
2 tablespoons soy sauce
1 tablespoon lime juice
1 teaspoon dark sesame oil
1 cup plain yogurt

1. Place 4 cups water in medium saucepan; bring to a boil over high heat. Drop cabbage leaves into water; cook 30 seconds. Drain. Rinse under cold water until cool; pat dry with paper towels.

2. Place remaining 1 cup water, ginger and red pepper flakes in medium saucepan; bring to a boil over high heat. Stir in couscous; cover. Remove saucepan from heat; let stand 5 minutes.

3. Place lamb, green onions and garlic in large skillet. Cook and stir over medium-high heat 5 minutes or until lamb is cooked through. Drain fat.

4. Combine couscous, lamb mixture, ¼ cup cilantro, soy sauce, lime juice and sesame oil in medium bowl. Spoon mixture evenly down centers of cabbage leaves. Fold ends of cabbage leaves over filling; roll up. Combine yogurt and remaining 2 tablespoons cilantro in small bowl; spoon evenly over rolls.   *Makes 16 servings*

pot stickers

Dipping Sauce (page 10 or 24)

2 cups all-purpose flour

¾ cup plus 2 tablespoons boiling water

½ cup finely chopped napa cabbage

½ pound ground pork

2 tablespoons finely chopped water chestnuts

1 green onion, finely chopped

1½ teaspoons cornstarch

1½ teaspoons rice wine or dry sherry

1½ teaspoons soy sauce

½ teaspoon minced fresh ginger

½ teaspoon dark sesame oil

¼ teaspoon sugar

2 tablespoons vegetable oil, divided

⅔ cup chicken broth, divided

1. Prepare Dipping Sauce; set aside.

2. Place flour in large bowl; make well in center. Pour in boiling water; stir with wooden spoon until dough forms.

3. Turn dough out onto lightly floured surface. Knead until smooth and satiny, about 5 minutes. Cover dough; let rest 30 minutes.

4. Squeeze cabbage to remove as much moisture as possible; place in large bowl. Add pork, water chestnuts, green onion, cornstarch, wine, soy sauce, ginger, sesame oil and sugar; mix well.

5. Divide dough in half; cover one half with plastic wrap. Roll out remaining half of dough to ⅛-inch thickness. Cut out 3-inch circles. Repeat with reserved half of dough.

6. Place 1 rounded teaspoon filling in center of each dough circle. Moisten edges with water; fold in half. Pinch edges together making pleats. Press dumpling down firmly, seam side up. Cover finished dumplings while shaping remaining dumplings. (Dumplings may be refrigerated for up to 4 hours or frozen in large resealable food storage bag.)

7. Heat 1 tablespoon vegetable oil in large nonstick skillet over medium heat. Place half of pot stickers in skillet, seam side up. (If cooking frozen dumplings, do not thaw.) Cook 5 to 6 minutes or until bottoms are golden brown.

8. Pour in ⅓ cup broth; cover tightly. Reduce heat to low. Simmer until all liquid is absorbed, about 10 minutes (15 minutes if frozen). Repeat with remaining vegetable oil, dumplings and broth. Serve with Dipping Sauce.   *Makes about 3 dozen*

 **Tip** You can make homemade pot stickers even if you don't have time to make the dough and roll it out. Just purchase wonton wrappers available in the refrigerated produce section of most markets. This time-saving trick is used even in many restaurant kitchens. Feel free to vary the filling to suit personal tastes as well. Pot stickers are delicious filled with seafood, any kind of ground meat or finely chopped vegetables.

19

mini egg rolls

½ pound ground pork

3 cloves garlic, minced

1 teaspoon minced fresh ginger

¼ teaspoon red pepper flakes

6 cups (12 ounces) shredded coleslaw mix

¼ cup soy sauce

1 tablespoon cornstarch

1 tablespoon seasoned rice vinegar

½ cup chopped green onions

28 wonton wrappers

Peanut or canola oil for frying

Sweet and sour sauce

Chinese hot mustard

1. Combine pork, garlic, ginger and red pepper flakes in large nonstick skillet; cook and stir over medium heat 4 minutes or until pork is cooked through, stirring to break up meat. Add coleslaw mix; cover and cook 2 minutes. Uncover and cook 2 minutes or until coleslaw mix is wilted but crisp-tender.

2. Combine soy sauce and cornstarch in small bowl; mix well. Stir into pork mixture. Add vinegar; cook 2 to 3 minutes or until sauce thickens. Remove from heat; stir in green onions.

3. To fill egg rolls, place wonton wrapper on clean work surface with one point facing you. Spoon level tablespoon pork mixture across and just below center of wrapper. Fold bottom point of wrapper up over filling; fold side points over filling, forming envelope shape. Moisten inside edges of top point with water and roll egg roll toward top point, pressing firmly to seal. Repeat with remaining wrappers and filling.

4. Heat about ¼ inch oil in large skillet over medium heat; fry egg rolls in small batches about 2 minutes per side or until golden brown. Drain on paper towels. Serve with sweet and sour sauce and hot mustard for dipping. *Makes 28 mini egg rolls*

thai salad rolls with spicy sweet & sour sauce

    Spicy Sweet & Sour Sauce (recipe follows)
 3 ounces thin rice noodles (rice vermicelli)
 ¼ pound large raw shrimp, peeled and deveined
 1 medium cucumber, peeled, seeded and cut into matchstick-size pieces
 ½ cup fresh cilantro leaves
 ½ cup fresh mint leaves
 1 large bunch green leaf lettuce or Boston bibb lettuce

1. Prepare Spicy Sweet & Sour Sauce; set aside. Soften noodles in medium bowl of hot water 20 to 30 minutes. Rinse under cold running water to cool; drain.

2. Meanwhile, bring water to a boil in medium saucepan. Add shrimp; return to a boil. Cook 3 to 5 minutes or until shrimp turn pink and opaque; drain. When cool, cut each shrimp lengthwise in half.

3. To assemble rolls, arrange shrimp, noodles, cucumber, cilantro and mint in center of lettuce leaves and roll up. Serve with Spicy Sweet & Sour Sauce.   *Makes 6 servings*

spicy sweet & sour sauce

 1 green onion
 1 tablespoon cornstarch
 2 tablespoons rice vinegar
 ¾ cup water
 ¼ cup packed brown sugar
 ½ teaspoon red pepper flakes
 2 tablespoons finely grated turnip

1. Finely chop white part of green onion; cut green portion into thin 1-inch strips. Reserve green strips for garnish. Combine cornstarch and vinegar in small bowl; mix well. Set aside.

2. Combine water, brown sugar, red pepper flakes and chopped green onion in small saucepan; bring to a boil. Stir in cornstarch mixture. Return to a boil; cook 1 minute or until sauce is clear and thickened. Cool. Sprinkle with turnip and reserved green onion strips just before serving.   *Makes about 1 cup*

steamed pork wontons with sweet soy dipping sauce

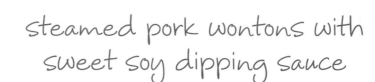

Wontons
- ½ pound ground pork
- ¼ cup chopped fresh cilantro
- 1½ tablespoons grated fresh ginger
- 1 teaspoon grated orange peel
- ¼ teaspoon ground red pepper
- ⅛ teaspoon salt
- 24 wonton wrappers
- 3 teaspoons vegetable oil
- 1 cup plus 3 tablespoons water, divided

Dipping Sauce
- 2 to 3 tablespoons sugar
- 2 tablespoons white vinegar
- 2 tablespoons lime juice
- 2 tablespoons soy sauce

1. Combine pork, cilantro, ginger, orange peel, red pepper and salt in medium bowl. Place rounded teaspoon in center of each wonton wrapper. Twist tops closed, using small amount of water to seal.

2. Heat 1½ teaspoons oil in large nonstick skillet over medium-high heat. Add 12 wontons and cook 1 minute or until golden brown on bottom. Add ½ cup water, cover; cook 5 minutes or until water has evaporated. Place on serving platter and cover with foil to keep warm. Repeat with remaining oil, wontons and water.

3. Combine sugar, vinegar, lime juice and soy sauce in small bowl. Microwave sauce on HIGH about 20 to 30 seconds, if desired. Serve with wontons. *Makes 24 wontons*

stir-fried mu shu pork wraps

1 tablespoon dark sesame oil

1 red bell pepper, cut into short thin strips

¾ pound pork tenderloin, cut into strips

1 medium zucchini or summer squash, or combination, cut into strips

3 cloves garlic, minced

2 cups coleslaw mix or shredded cabbage

2 tablespoons hoisin sauce

4 (10-inch) wraps

¼ cup plum sauce

1. Heat sesame oil in large deep nonstick skillet over medium-high heat. Add bell pepper; stir-fry 2 minutes. Add pork, zucchini and garlic; stir-fry 4 to 5 minutes or until pork is cooked through and vegetables are crisp-tender. Add coleslaw mix; stir-fry 2 minutes or until wilted. Add hoisin sauce; cook and stir 1 minute.

2. Heat wraps according to package directions. Spread plum sauce down centers of wraps; top with pork mixture. Roll up tightly; cut diagonally in half.

Makes 4 servings

Tip Hoisin sauce is made of soybeans, garlic, chile peppers and spices. The flavor is a distinctive blend of salty, spicy and sweet. Hoisin is easy to find in the Asian aisle of most supermarkets in either bottles or cans. After opening, refrigerate bottled hoisin sauces. Canned hoisin should be transferred to a non-metallic container before refrigerating.

26

asian lettuce wraps

2 teaspoons canola oil

1½ pounds boneless skinless chicken breast or pork shoulder, chopped

2 leeks, chopped

1 cup shiitake mushrooms, stems removed and caps chopped

1 stalk celery, chopped

2 tablespoons water

1 tablespoon oyster sauce

1 tablespoon soy sauce

1 teaspoon dark sesame oil

¼ teaspoon ground black pepper

1 package (8 ounces) coleslaw or broccoli slaw mix

½ red bell pepper, cut into thin strips

½ pound raw shrimp, peeled and chopped

3 tablespoons salted dry roasted peanuts, coarsely chopped

Hoisin sauce, to taste

10 to 15 leaves romaine lettuce, ribs removed

Fresh chives (optional)

Slow Cooker Directions

1. Heat canola oil in small skillet over medium-high heat. Add chicken; cook and stir until browned. Transfer to slow cooker. Add leeks, mushrooms, celery, water, oyster sauce, soy sauce, sesame oil and black pepper. Toss slaw and bell pepper in medium bowl; place in slow cooker.

2. Cover; cook on LOW 4 to 5 hours or on HIGH 2 to 2½ hours. Stir in shrimp for last 20 minutes of cooking until pink and opaque. Transfer mixture to large bowl; mix in peanuts.

3. Spread hoisin sauce on lettuce leaf. Add 1 to 2 tablespoons meat mixture and roll up. Tie with chives, if desired.

Makes 5 to 6 servings

shrimp dumplings with black bean coffee sauce

Dumplings

½ pound medium raw shrimp, peeled and deveined

1 teaspoon grated fresh ginger

2 green onions, thinly sliced

1 tablespoon soy sauce

1 teaspoon dark sesame oil

1 can (5 ounces) water chestnuts, drained and chopped

1 can (5 ounces) bamboo shoots, drained and chopped

¼ cup fresh cilantro

¼ cup fresh basil

1 package wonton wrappers

Black Bean Coffee Sauce

1 teaspoon dark sesame oil

½ cup brewed coffee

4 tablespoons bottled black bean with garlic sauce

½ teaspoon hoisin sauce

1. Place shrimp, ginger, green onions, soy sauce and 1 tablespoon sesame oil in food processor or blender; pulse until paste forms. Add water chestnuts, bamboo shoots, cilantro and basil; pulse briefly.

2. Place wonton wrapper on work surface. Place 1 heaping teaspoon shrimp mixture into center. Fold wrapper over filling to form triangle; moisten edges with water and press to seal. Repeat with remaining wrappers and filling.

3. Place steamer insert into large saucepan. Pour water into saucepan to just below steamer. Spray steamer with nonstick cooking spray. Bring water to a boil.

4. Heat 1 teaspoon sesame oil in small saucepan. Add coffee, black bean sauce and hoisin sauce; stir until combined. Remove from heat and keep warm.

5. Place dumplings in steamer in single layer without crowding. Cover; steam 8 minutes or until filling is cooked through and dough is shiny and translucent.

6. Serve with Black Bean Coffee Sauce.   *Makes about 36 dumplings*

moo shu vegetables

6 or 7 dried shiitake mushrooms (about ½ ounce)
2 tablespoons vegetable oil
2 cloves garlic, minced
2 cups shredded napa cabbage
1 red bell pepper, cut into short, thin strips
1 cup fresh bean sprouts
2 green onions, cut into short, thin strips
1 tablespoon teriyaki sauce
⅓ cup plum sauce
8 (6-inch) flour tortillas, warmed

1. Soak mushrooms in warm water 20 minutes. Drain; squeeze out excess water. Discard stems; slice caps.

2. Heat oil in wok or large nonstick skillet over medium heat. Add garlic; stir-fry 30 seconds.

3. Add cabbage, mushrooms and bell pepper; stir-fry 3 minutes. Add bean sprouts and green onions; stir-fry 2 minutes. Add teriyaki sauce; stir-fry 30 seconds.

4. Spread about 2 teaspoons plum sauce on each tortilla. Spoon heaping ¼ cup of vegetable mixture over sauce. Fold bottom of each tortilla up over filling, then fold sides over filling.

Makes 8 servings

 **Tip** Dried shiitake mushrooms are sometimes called Chinese black mushrooms. They need to be soaked before using since they are woody and hard. You may discard the tough stems or save them to flavor a stock or sauce. If you wish to use the soaking water for a soup or sauce, strain it first through a fine mesh sieve to remove any dirt or grit.

Cool & Crisp

Salads just became a lot more interesting. These Asian-inspired recipes show off crunchy ingredients like bok choy and snow peas and punch up flavor with sweet and spicy dressings.

mandarin chicken salad

3½ ounces thin rice noodles (rice vermicelli)
1 can (6 ounces) mandarin orange segments, chilled
⅓ cup honey
2 tablespoons rice vinegar
2 tablespoons soy sauce
1 can (8 ounces) sliced water chestnuts, drained
4 cups shredded napa cabbage
1 cup shredded red cabbage
½ cup sliced radishes
4 thin slices red onion, cut in half and separated
¾ pound boneless skinless chicken breasts, cooked and cut into strips

1. Soften rice noodles in large bowl of hot water 20 to 30 minutes or according to package directions. Drain and set aside. Drain mandarin orange segments, reserving ⅓ cup liquid. Whisk together reserved liquid, honey, vinegar and soy sauce in small bowl. Add water chestnuts.

2. Arrange rice noodles on serving platter. Top evenly with napa and red cabbages, radishes and onion. Top with chicken and orange segments. Remove water chestnuts from dressing and arrange on salads. Drizzle with remaining dressing.

Makes 4 servings

Prep and Cook Time: 20 minutes

thai grilled beef salad

3 tablespoons Thai seasoning, divided
1 beef flank steak (about 1 pound)
2 tablespoons chopped fresh cilantro
2 tablespoons chopped fresh basil
2 red Thai peppers *or* 1 red jalapeño pepper,* seeded and slivered
1 tablespoon finely chopped lemongrass
1 tablespoon minced red onion
1 clove garlic, minced
  Juice of 1 lime
1 tablespoon fish sauce
1 large carrot, grated
1 cucumber, chopped
4 cups assorted salad greens

*Thai chili peppers and jalapeño peppers can sting and irritate the skin, so wear rubber gloves when handling peppers and do not touch your eyes.

1. Prepare grill for direct cooking.

2. Sprinkle 1 tablespoon Thai seasoning over both sides of beef; turn to coat. Cover and marinate 15 minutes. Place steak on grid over medium heat. Grill, uncovered, 20 minutes for medium or until desired doneness, turning once. Cool 10 minutes.

3. Meanwhile, combine remaining 2 tablespoons Thai seasoning, cilantro, basil, peppers, lemongrass, red onion, garlic, lime juice and fish sauce in medium bowl; mix well.

4. Thinly slice beef across grain. Add beef, carrot and cucumber to dressing; toss to coat. Arrange on bed of greens.

Makes 4 servings

marinated cucumbers

1 large cucumber (about 12 ounces)
2 tablespoons rice vinegar
2 tablespoons peanut or vegetable oil
2 tablespoons soy sauce
1½ teaspoons sugar
1 clove garlic, minced
¼ teaspoon red pepper flakes
Red bell pepper strips (optional)

1. Score cucumber lengthwise with tines of fork. Cut in half lengthwise; scrape out and discard seeds. Cut crosswise into ⅛-inch slices; place in medium bowl.

2. Combine rice vinegar, oil, soy sauce, sugar, garlic and red pepper flakes in small bowl. Pour over cucumber and toss to coat. Cover; refrigerate at least 4 hours or up to 2 days. Garnish with bell pepper strips. *Makes 4 to 6 servings*

38

 Tip There are many varieties of rice vinegar used in Asian cuisine. Some are labeled rice wine vinegar. Both Chinese and Japanese rice vinegar are made from fermented rice. They are milder and less acidic than ordinary white vinegar. Seasoned rice vinegar is a Japanese vinegar flavored with salt and sugar and often used to prepare sushi rice. Chinese black vinegar is used mainly as a table condiment. It has a slightly sweet flavor similar to balsamic vinegar.

seared asian steak salad

¾ pound boneless beef sirloin steak
(¾ inch thick)

2 tablespoons soy sauce

3 tablespoons hoisin sauce

2 tablespoons packed dark brown
sugar

1 teaspoon grated orange peel

2 tablespoons orange juice

2 tablespoons cider vinegar

2 teaspoons dark sesame oil

1 teaspoon grated fresh ginger

⅛ teaspoon dried red pepper flakes
Nonstick cooking spray

1 bag (5 ounces) spring greens

½ cup thinly sliced red onion

1 cup thinly sliced red bell pepper

1 cup snow peas

1 medium carrot, cut into matchstick-size pieces

1. Place beef and soy sauce in large resealable food storage bag; seal bag and turn to coat. Marinate in refrigerator 2 hours or up to 24 hours, turning several times.

2. For dressing, combine hoisin sauce, brown sugar, orange peel, orange juice, vinegar, sesame oil, ginger and red pepper flakes in small bowl; set aside.

3. Spray large nonstick skillet with cooking spray and heat over medium heat. Remove beef from marinade; discard marinade. Add beef to skillet; cook 6 to 8 minutes or until desired doneness, turning once. Place beef on cutting board; let stand 3 minutes before thinly slicing.

4. Arrange greens, onion, bell pepper, snow peas and carrot on serving plates. Whisk dressing until well blended; drizzle over salads. Top with beef. *Makes 4 servings*

szechuan chicken salad with peanut dressing

1 pound boneless skinless chicken breasts

1 can (about 14 ounces) chicken broth

1 tablespoon creamy peanut butter

1 tablespoon peanut or vegetable oil

1 tablespoon soy sauce

1 tablespoon rice vinegar

1 teaspoon dark sesame oil

¼ teaspoon ground red pepper

Shredded lettuce

Chopped fresh cilantro or green onions (optional)

1. Place chicken in single layer in large skillet. Pour broth over chicken; bring to a boil over high heat. Reduce heat to medium-low. Cover; simmer 10 to 12 minutes or until chicken is no longer pink in center.

2. Meanwhile, mix peanut butter and peanut oil in small bowl until smooth. Stir in soy sauce, vinegar, sesame oil and red pepper.

3. Drain chicken, reserving 2 tablespoons broth.* Set chicken aside to cool. Slice, shred or coarsely chop chicken. Stir reserved broth into peanut butter mixture.

4. Arrange chicken on lettuce-lined plates. Serve salad with peanut dressing. Sprinkle with cilantro.   *Makes 4 servings*

Strain remaining broth; cover and refrigerate or freeze for use in other recipes.

41

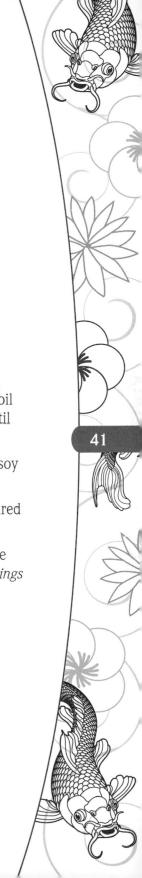

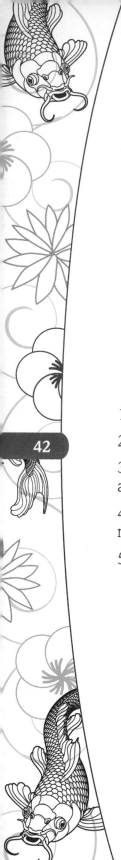

asian tofu salad

½ (14-ounce) package extra firm tofu, drained
4 tablespoons rice vinegar
3 tablespoons soy sauce
1½ tablespoons sugar
1 tablespoon dark sesame oil
1 to 2 teaspoons chili garlic sauce
1 teaspoon grated ginger
1 cup snow peas, trimmed
8 cups mixed salad greens
2 medium carrots, julienned
1 medium cucumber, thinly sliced
¼ cup unsalted dry roasted peanuts, coarsely chopped (optional)

1. Cut tofu into ½-inch cubes; drain in single layer on kitchen towel.

2. Combine vinegar, soy sauce, sugar, sesame oil, chili sauce and ginger in small bowl.

3. Heat nonstick skillet over medium-high heat; add tofu, 2 tablespoons sauce mixture and snow peas. Cook and stir 5 to 7 minutes. Let cool slightly.

4. Place mixed greens in salad bowl and add carrots and cucumbers. Drizzle with remaining sauce mixture; toss to mix.

5. Add warm tofu mixture and peanuts, if desired.

Makes 5 servings

chinese crab & cucumber salad

1 large cucumber, peeled

¾ pound crabmeat (fresh, pasteurized or thawed frozen), flaked*

½ red bell pepper, diced

½ cup mayonnaise

3 tablespoons soy sauce

1 tablespoon dark sesame oil

1 teaspoon ground ginger

½ pound bean sprouts

1 tablespoon sesame seeds, toasted**

Fresh chives, chopped

Pick out and discard any shell or cartilage from crabmeat.

**To toast sesame seeds, spread in small skillet. Shake skillet over medium-low heat about 3 minutes or until seeds begin to pop and turn golden.*

1. Cut cucumber in half lengthwise; scoop out seeds. Slice into ½-inch pieces. Combine cucumber, crabmeat and bell pepper in large bowl.

2. Whisk mayonnaise, soy sauce, sesame oil and ginger in small bowl until blended. Add to crabmeat mixture; toss to coat. Refrigerate 1 hour to allow flavors to blend.

3. To serve, arrange bean sprouts on serving plates. Spoon crabmeat mixture on top; sprinkle with sesame seeds and chives.

Makes 4 main-dish servings

44

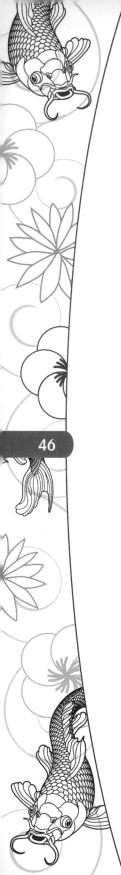

bright and gingery chinese slaw

½ cup peanuts

2 cups matchstick-size carrots

½ cup thinly shredded red cabbage

1 medium red bell pepper, cut into thin 2-inch strips

½ medium green bell pepper, cut into thin 2-inch strips

3 tablespoons sugar

3 tablespoons soy sauce

2 to 3 tablespoons cider vinegar

2 tablespoons dark sesame oil

1 tablespoon grated fresh ginger

¼ teaspoon red pepper flakes

1. Heat medium skillet over medium-high heat. Add peanuts; cook and stir 3 minutes or until lightly browned; set aside to cool.

2. Combine carrots, cabbage and bell peppers in medium bowl.

3. Combine sugar, soy sauce, vinegar, oil, ginger and red pepper flakes in jar. Secure lid tightly; shake vigorously until well blended. Pour over carrot mixture. Add peanuts. Toss to coat completely.   *Makes 6 servings*

Variation: Sprinkle with 1 tablespoon sesame seeds; mix well. If the flavor of sesame oil is too strong, substitute 1 tablespoon canola oil for 1 tablespoon sesame oil.

thai broccoli salad

¼ cup creamy or chunky peanut butter

2 tablespoons EQUAL® SPOONFUL*

1½ tablespoons hot water

1 tablespoon lime juice

1 tablespoon light soy sauce

1½ teaspoons dark sesame oil

¼ teaspoon red pepper flakes

2 tablespoons vegetable oil

3 cups fresh broccoli florets

½ cup chopped red bell pepper

¼ cup sliced green onions

1 clove garlic, crushed

May substitute 3 packets EQUAL® sweetener.

• Combine peanut butter, Equal®, hot water, lime juice, soy sauce, sesame oil and red pepper flakes until well blended; set aside.

• Heat vegetable oil in large skillet over medium-high heat. Add broccoli, red pepper, green onions and garlic. Stir-fry 3 to 4 minutes until vegetables are tender-crisp. Remove from heat and stir in peanut butter mixture.

• Serve warm or at room temperature.   *Makes 4 servings*

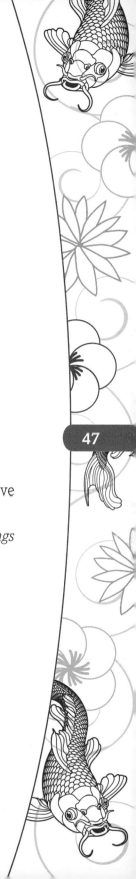

47

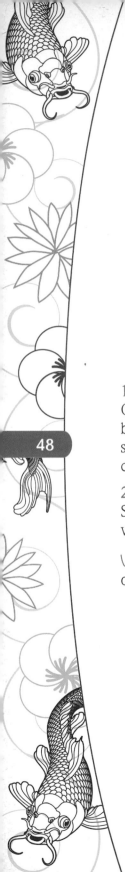

spicy oriental shrimp salad

    1 head iceberg lettuce
  ½ cup fresh basil leaves
  ¼ cup rice vinegar
    1 piece fresh ginger (2 inches), peeled
    1 tablespoon soy sauce
    3 cloves garlic
    2 teaspoons dark sesame oil
    1 teaspoon red pepper flakes
  28 large raw shrimp, peeled and deveined, tails on
    1 to 2 limes, cut into wedges (optional)
      Vinaigrette Dressing (recipe follows)

1. Core, rinse and thoroughly drain lettuce. Refrigerate in airtight container to crisp. Combine basil, vinegar, ginger, soy sauce, garlic, sesame oil and red pepper flakes in blender or food processor. Blend to form rough paste, using on/off pulsing action, scraping sides as needed. Transfer paste to large mixing bowl. Add shrimp; stir until coated. Cover and refrigerate 2 hours or overnight.

2. Preheat broiler. Broil shrimp 4 minutes or until pink and opaque, turning once. Shred lettuce; arrange on four plates. Top with cooked shrimp. Garnish with lime wedges. Serve with Vinaigrette Dressing. *Makes 4 servings*

Vinaigrette Dressing: Whisk 3 tablespoons red wine vinegar with 1½ tablespoons olive oil in small bowl until blended.

chinese chicken salad

4 cups chopped bok choy

3 cups diced cooked chicken breast

1 cup shredded carrots

2 tablespoons minced fresh chives or green onions

2 tablespoons hot chili garlic sauce

1½ tablespoons peanut or canola oil

1 tablespoon balsamic vinegar

1 tablespoon soy sauce

1 teaspoon minced fresh ginger

1. Place bok choy, chicken, carrots and chives in large bowl.

2. Combine chili garlic sauce, oil, vinegar, soy sauce and ginger in small bowl; mix well. Pour over chicken mixture; toss gently. *Makes 4 servings*

50

Tip Chili garlic sauce is a condiment found in some form in every Asian cuisine. It is made from a variety of dried or fresh chile peppers plus garlic, oil and sometimes sugar that are ground into a paste. The level of heat varies and names change depending on ethnicity. Sriracha (which means rooster) sauce is the Vietnamese version. Sambal Oelek is Indonesian in origin. Chinese chili garlic is usually just labeled chili garlic. They can be used interchangeably, so find the kind that pleases your palate.

summer szechuan tofu salad

¼ cup soy sauce
 1 tablespoon canola or peanut oil
 1 tablespoon dark sesame oil
 1 teaspoon minced fresh ginger
½ teaspoon hot pepper sauce or more to taste
 1 package (14 ounces) extra firm tofu
 4 cups baby spinach leaves
 4 cups sliced napa cabbage
 2 cups halved snow peas
 1 cup matchstick-size carrots
 1 cup fresh bean sprouts
¼ cup dry-roasted peanuts or toasted slivered almonds
    Chopped cilantro or green onions (optional)

1. Combine soy sauce, canola oil, sesame oil, ginger and hot pepper sauce in small bowl. Drain tofu and place between two paper towels. Press lightly to drain excess water from tofu. Cut tofu into 1-inch cubes. Place in shallow dish. Drizzle 2 tablespoons soy sauce mixture over tofu.

2. Combine spinach, cabbage, snow peas, carrots and bean sprouts in large bowl. Add remaining soy sauce mixture. Toss well. Transfer to plates. Top with tofu mixture, peanuts and cilantro, if desired.

Makes 4 servings

chicken and cucumber salad (goi ga tom)

1 quart plus 3 tablespoons water, divided
3 chicken thighs (about 1 pound)
2 medium cucumbers, cut in half lengthwise, seeded and thinly sliced
1 large carrot, cut into matchstick-size strips
1 teaspoon salt
2 tablespoons fish sauce
1½ tablespoons sugar
1½ tablespoons fresh lime juice
1 clove garlic, finely chopped
½ cup roasted unsalted peanuts, finely chopped
1 tablespoon chopped fresh cilantro
1 tablespoon chopped fresh mint leaves
1 tablespoon chopped fresh basil
1 tablespoon chopped green onion
8 jumbo cooked shrimp, peeled and deveined

54

1. Bring 1 quart water in medium saucepan to a boil over high heat. Add chicken. Reduce heat to low; simmer, covered, 25 minutes or until cooked through. Drain; let stand until cool enough to handle. Skin and debone chicken; cut into ¼-inch pieces.

2. Meanwhile, combine cucumbers and carrot in large bowl; sprinkle with salt. Toss to mix well; let stand 15 minutes.

3. For dressing, combine remaining 3 tablespoons water, fish sauce, sugar, lime juice and garlic in small bowl; stir until sugar is dissolved.

4. Squeeze cucumber mixture to extract liquid; discard liquid.

5. Combine cucumber mixture, chicken and peanuts in medium bowl; drizzle with dressing. Toss to coat; refrigerate, covered, 30 minutes to 2 hours.

6. Mix cilantro, mint, basil and green onion in small bowl.

7. Transfer salad mixture to serving dish. Garnish with shrimp; sprinkle with mixed herbs.

Makes 4 servings

sesame rice salad

1 can (15 ounces) mandarin orange segments, undrained
1 teaspoon ground ginger
2 cups MINUTE® Brown Rice, uncooked
½ cup Asian sesame salad dressing
3 green onions, thinly sliced
1 can (8 ounces) sliced water chestnuts, drained and chopped
½ cup celery, sliced

Drain oranges, reserving liquid. Add enough water to reserved liquid to measure 1¾ cups. Stir in ginger.

Prepare rice according to package directions, substituting 1¾ cups orange liquid for water. Place in large bowl. Refrigerate 30 minutes.

Add dressing, green onions, water chestnuts and celery; mix lightly. Gently stir in oranges.

Makes 4 servings

56

 Tip Water chestnuts are not really nuts—they're the edible tuber of a Southeast Asian water plant. Their mild, slightly sweet flavor and firm crunch make them a wonderful addition to salads and stir-fries. While most water chestnuts are sold canned, fresh water chestnuts are often available in Asian markets. They have a dark brown skin that must be peeled off and a crunchy white interior that is a touch sweeter than the canned version.

Bowls & Skewers

From Chinese Hot and Sour Soup to Korean Kalbitang, Asian soups are mouthwatering and satisfying meals in a bowl. You'll find classic kabob recipes too, along with a variety of delightful dipping sauces.

hot and sour soup

3 cans (about 14 ounces each) chicken broth
½ pound boneless skinless chicken breasts, cut into strips
1 cup shredded carrots
1 cup thinly sliced mushrooms
½ cup bamboo shoots, cut into strips
2 tablespoons rice vinegar or white wine vinegar
½ to ¾ teaspoon white pepper
¼ to ½ teaspoon hot pepper sauce
2 tablespoons cornstarch
2 tablespoons soy sauce
1 tablespoon rice wine or dry sherry
2 medium green onions, sliced
1 egg, lightly beaten

1. Combine broth, chicken, carrots, mushrooms, bamboo shoots, vinegar, white pepper and hot pepper sauce in large saucepan. Bring to a boil over medium-high heat; reduce heat to low. Cover and simmer 5 minutes or until chicken is cooked through.

2. Blend cornstarch, soy sauce and wine in small bowl until smooth. Add to chicken broth mixture. Cook and stir until mixture comes to a boil. Stir in green onions and egg. Cook 1 minute, stirring in one direction, until egg is cooked.   *Makes 7 servings*

thai-style pork kabobs

⅓ cup soy sauce

2 tablespoons fresh lime juice

2 tablespoons water

2 teaspoons hot chili oil*

2 cloves garlic, minced

1 teaspoon minced fresh ginger

¾ pound pork tenderloin

1 red or yellow bell pepper, cut into pieces

1 red or sweet onion, cut into chunks

2 cups hot cooked rice

*If hot chili oil is not available, combine 2 teaspoons vegetable oil and ½ teaspoon red pepper flakes in small microwavable cup. Microwave at HIGH 30 to 45 seconds. Let stand 5 minutes to allow flavor to develop.

1. Combine soy sauce, lime juice, water, chili oil, garlic and ginger in medium bowl. Reserve ⅓ cup mixture for dipping sauce; set aside.

2. Cut pork tenderloin into ½-inch strips. Add to bowl with soy sauce mixture; toss to coat. Cover; refrigerate at least 30 minutes or up to 2 hours, stirring once.

3. Spray grid with nonstick cooking spray. Prepare grill for direct cooking. If using wooden skewers, soak in water 20 minutes before using to prevent burning.

4. Remove pork from marinade; discard marinade. Alternately thread pork strips, bell pepper and onion onto skewers.

5. Grill, covered, over medium-high heat 6 to 8 minutes or until pork is cooked through, turning once. Serve with rice and reserved dipping sauce.

Makes 4 servings

noodles with simmered chicken

4 dried shiitake mushrooms

1 boneless skinless chicken breast, thinly sliced

2 teaspoons rice wine or dry sherry

1 small bunch watercress

8 ounces thin Chinese wheat noodles (mein)

2 cups chicken broth

1 tablespoon soy sauce

¼ cup sliced bamboo shoots

1 teaspoon dark sesame oil

Dash white pepper

2 green onions, thinly sliced

1. Place mushrooms in bowl and cover with hot water. Let stand 30 minutes. Drain and squeeze out excess water. Cut off and discard stems; cut caps into thin slices.

2. Place chicken slices in medium bowl; sprinkle with wine. Let stand 15 minutes.

3. Wash watercress and discard thick stems.

4. Cook noodles according to package directions until tender but firm. Drain, rinse under cold running water and drain again.

5. Bring broth and soy sauce to a boil in large saucepan. Add mushrooms, chicken and bamboo shoots. Reduce heat and simmer 4 minutes or until chicken is cooked through. Add watercress, sesame oil and pepper; simmer 1 minute. Add noodles and cook until heated through.

6. Divide noodles, chicken and vegetables between two serving bowls. Ladle broth over noodles. Sprinkle each serving with green onions. *Makes 2 servings*

shrimp, mushroom and omelet soup

10 to 12 dried shiitake mushrooms (about 1 ounce)
3 eggs
1 tablespoon chopped fresh chives or minced green onion
2 teaspoons vegetable oil
3 cans (about 14 ounces each) reduced-sodium chicken broth
2 tablespoons oyster sauce
¾ pound medium raw shrimp, peeled and deveined
3 cups lightly packed fresh spinach, stemmed
1 tablespoon lime juice
Red pepper flakes

1. Place mushrooms in bowl; cover with hot water. Let stand 30 minutes or until softened.

2. Meanwhile, whisk eggs and chives in small bowl until blended. Heat oil in large nonstick skillet over medium-high heat. Pour egg mixture into pan. Reduce heat to medium; cover and cook, without stirring, 2 minutes or until set on bottom. Slide spatula under omelet; lift omelet and tilt pan to allow uncooked egg to flow under. Repeat at several places around omelet.

3. Slide omelet onto flat plate. Hold another plate over omelet and turn over. Slide omelet back into skillet; cook 20 seconds. Slide back onto plate. When cool enough to handle, roll up omelet; cut into ¼-inch-wide strips.

4. Drain mushrooms; squeeze out excess water. Remove and discard stems. Slice caps into thin strips.

5. Combine mushrooms, broth and oyster sauce in large saucepan. Cover and bring to a boil. Reduce heat to low; cook 5 minutes. Increase heat to medium-high; add shrimp and cook 2 minutes or until pink and opaque. Add omelet strips and spinach; remove from heat. Cover and let stand 1 to 2 minutes or until spinach wilts slightly. Stir in lime juice and red pepper flakes.

Makes 6 servings

short rib soup (kalbitang)

2 tablespoons Sesame Salt (page 67)

2 pounds beef short ribs or flanken-style ribs

2 quarts water

2 tablespoons dried cloud ear or other Asian mushrooms

½ cup thinly sliced green onions

3 tablespoons soy sauce

2 cloves garlic, cut into slivers (1 tablespoon)

½ teaspoon dark sesame oil

¼ teaspoon red pepper flakes

Nonstick cooking spray

1 egg, lightly beaten

1 bunch chives, chopped

1. Prepare Sesame Salt; set aside.

2. Score both sides of short ribs in diamond pattern with tip of sharp knife.

3. Bring ribs and water to a boil in Dutch oven over high heat. Reduce heat to medium; frequently skim foam that rises to surface until broth is clear. Reduce heat to medium-low; cook, uncovered, about 1½ hours or until meat is tender. Remove ribs from broth; let cool slightly.

4. Place mushrooms in bowl; cover with hot water. Let stand 30 minutes or until caps are soft.

5. Drain mushrooms; squeeze out excess water. Remove and discard stems. Cut caps into thin slices.

6. To degrease broth, let stand 5 minutes to allow fat to rise. Quickly pull paper towel across surface of broth, allowing towel to absorb fat. Repeat with clean paper towels as many times as necessary to remove all fat. (If time allows, refrigerate broth for several hours or overnight and remove fat that rises to surface.)

7. Place ribs on cutting board. Cut meat from bones; discard bones and gristle. Cut meat into bite-size pieces.

8. Combine beef, mushrooms, green onions, soy sauce, Sesame Salt, garlic, sesame oil and red pepper flakes in medium bowl. Add beef mixture to broth; cook 15 minutes over medium-low heat.

9. Meanwhile, spray small skillet with nonstick cooking spray. Pour egg into pan; cook over medium-high heat until set on both sides. Let cool.

10. Cut omelet into strips. Garnish soup with omelet strips and chives.

Makes 4 servings

Sesame Salt

½ cup sesame seeds
¼ teaspoon salt

1. Place seeds in large skillet. Shake skillet over medium-low heat about 4 to 6 minutes or until seeds begin to pop and turn golden. Set aside to cool.

2. Crush toasted sesame seeds and salt with mortar and pestle or process in clean coffee or spice grinder. Refrigerate in covered glass jar for use in additional Korean recipes.

Makes ½ cup

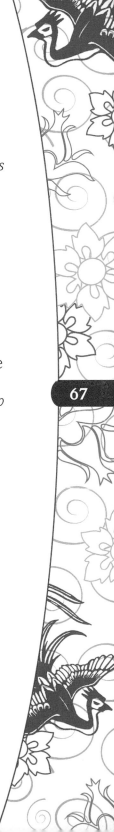

szechuan grilled mushrooms

1 pound large fresh cremini mushrooms
2 tablespoons soy sauce
2 teaspoons peanut or vegetable oil
1 teaspoon dark sesame oil
1 clove garlic, minced
½ teaspoon crushed Szechuan peppercorns or red pepper flakes

1. Place mushrooms in large resealable food storage bag. Add soy sauce, peanut oil, sesame oil, garlic and peppercorns to bag. Seal bag; shake to coat. Marinate at room temperature 15 minutes.

2. Thread mushrooms onto skewers.* Grill or broil mushrooms 5 inches from heat 10 minutes or until lightly browned, turning once. Serve immediately.

Makes 4 servings

If using wooden skewers, soak in water 20 minutes before using to prevent burning.

Variation: Add 4 green onions, cut into 1½-inch pieces, to marinade. Thread onto skewers with mushrooms. Grill or broil as directed in step 2.

Tip Szechuan peppercorns are not related to black pepper or to chile peppers despite their English name. These reddish brown spices are actually tiny seedpods and are usually crushed before using. The flavor has hints of lemon, and while they are not hot like a hot red pepper, Szechuan peppercorns produce a tingly, slightly numbing sensation on the tongue.

thai roasted squash soup

2 tablespoons vegetable oil

2 teaspoons curry powder

1 butternut squash, peeled, seeded and cut into 2-inch pieces (about 6 cups)

1 large sweet onion, cut into eighths

1 tablespoon chopped fresh ginger root

3 cups SWANSON® Chicken Broth (Regular, Natural Goodness® or Certified Organic)

1 can (15 ounces) cream of coconut

3 tablespoons chopped fresh cilantro leaves

1. Heat the oven to 425°F.

2. Stir the oil and curry in a large bowl. Add the squash and onion and toss to coat. Spread the vegetables onto a 17×11-inch roasting pan.

3. Bake for 25 minutes or until the vegetables are golden brown, stirring occasionally.

4. Heat the vegetables, ginger root, broth and cream of coconut in a 4-quart saucepan over medium-high heat to a boil. Reduce the heat to low. Cook for 20 minutes or until the vegetables are tender.

5. Spoon ⅓ of the vegetable mixture into a blender or food processor. Cover and blend until smooth. Pour the mixture into a large bowl. Repeat the blending process twice more with the remaining vegetable mixture. Return all of the puréed mixture to the saucepan. Cook over medium heat until the mixture is hot. Season to taste. Divide the soup among 6 serving bowls. Sprinkle with the cilantro.   *Makes 6 servings*

Prep Time: 35 minutes
Cook Time: 50 minutes
Total Time: 1 hour 25 minutes

70

tofu satay with peanut sauce

Satay

    1 package (about 14 ounces) firm tofu, drained and pressed*
    ⅓ cup water
    ⅓ cup soy sauce
    1 tablespoon dark sesame oil
    1 teaspoon minced garlic
    1 teaspoon minced ginger
   24 white button mushrooms, trimmed
    1 large red bell pepper, cut into 12 pieces

Peanut Sauce

    1 can (about 14 ounces) unsweetened coconut milk
    ½ cup smooth peanut butter
    2 tablespoons packed brown sugar
    1 tablespoon rice vinegar
    1 to 2 teaspoons red Thai curry paste

To press tofu, cut in half horizontally. Place tofu between layers of paper towels. Place flat, heavy object on top for 10 to 30 minutes.

1. Cut tofu into 24 cubes.

2. Combine water, soy sauce, sesame oil, garlic and ginger in large resealable food storage bag. Add tofu cubes, mushrooms and bell pepper; seal bag. Turn to coat. Marinate 30 minutes, turning occasionally. Soak eight 8-inch bamboo skewers in water 20 minutes.

3. Preheat oven to 400°F. Drain tofu mixture; discard marinade. Thread vegetables and tofu onto skewers.

4. Spray 13×9-inch baking pan with nonstick cooking spray. Place skewers in baking pan. Bake 25 minutes or until tofu cubes are lightly browned and vegetables are softened.

5. Meanwhile, whisk coconut milk, peanut butter, brown sugar, vinegar and curry paste in small saucepan over medium heat. Bring to a boil, stirring constantly. Reduce heat to low; cook 20 minutes or until creamy and thick, stirring often. Serve satay with sauce.

Makes 4 servings

japanese noodle soup

1 package (8½ ounces) udon noodles
1 teaspoon vegetable oil
1 medium red bell pepper, cut into thin strips
1 medium carrot, diagonally sliced
2 green onions, thinly sliced
2 cans (about 14 ounces each) reduced-sodium beef broth
1 cup water
1 teaspoon soy sauce
½ teaspoon grated fresh ginger
½ teaspoon black pepper
2 cups thinly sliced fresh shiitake mushrooms, stems discarded
4 ounces daikon (Japanese radish), peeled and cut into thin strips
4 ounces firm tofu, drained and cut into ½-inch cubes

1. Cook noodles according to package directions; drain. Rinse; set aside.

2. Heat oil in large nonstick saucepan over medium-high heat. Add bell pepper, carrot and green onions; cook about 3 minutes or until slightly softened. Stir in broth, water, soy sauce, ginger and black pepper; bring to a boil. Add mushrooms, daikon and tofu; reduce heat and simmer 5 minutes.

3. Place noodles in serving dishes; ladle soup over noodles.   *Makes 6 servings*

73

egg drop soup

4 cups chicken broth

2 tablespoons soy sauce

1 tablespoon rice wine or dry sherry

1 tablespoon cornstarch

1 tablespoon water

2 eggs, well beaten

2 green onions, thinly sliced

2 teaspoons dark sesame oil

1. Combine broth, soy sauce and wine in large saucepan; bring to a boil over high heat. Reduce heat to low; simmer 2 minutes.

2. Blend cornstarch and water in small bowl until smooth. Stir into soup until blended. Simmer 3 minutes or until slightly thickened.

3. Slowly add eggs to soup in thin stream, stirring constantly in one direction. Stir in green onions. Remove from heat; stir in sesame oil. Serve immediately.

Makes 4 servings

chicken kabobs with thai dipping sauce

1 pound boneless skinless chicken breasts, cut into 1-inch cubes
1 small cucumber, seeded and cut into small chunks
1 cup cherry tomatoes
2 green onions, cut into 1-inch pieces
⅔ cup teriyaki baste & glaze sauce
⅓ cup FRANK'S® REDHOT® Original Cayenne Pepper Sauce
⅓ cup peanut butter
3 tablespoons frozen orange juice concentrate, undiluted
2 cloves garlic, minced

Thread chicken, cucumber, tomatoes and onions alternately onto skewers; set aside.

To prepare Thai Dipping Sauce, combine teriyaki baste & glaze sauce, Frank's RedHot Sauce, peanut butter, orange juice concentrate and garlic; mix well. Reserve ⅔ cup sauce for dipping.

Brush skewers with some of remaining sauce. Place skewers on oiled grid. Grill over hot coals 10 minutes or until chicken is no longer pink in center, turning and basting often with remaining sauce. Serve skewers with reserved Thai Dipping Sauce. Garnish as desired.

Makes 6 appetizer servings

Prep Time: 15 minutes
Cook Time: 10 minutes

76

miso soup with tofu

½ cup dried bonito flakes*

4 cups chicken broth

2 teaspoons vegetable oil

1 leek, finely chopped

1 tablespoon white miso**

8 ounces firm tofu, cut into ½-inch cubes (about 1½ cups)

*If dried bonito flakes (katsuobushi) are unavailable, use all chicken broth and add an additional 1 tablespoon miso.

**A fermented soybean paste used frequently in Japanese cooking. Miso comes in many varieties; the light yellow miso, usually labeled "white", is the mildest. Look for it in tubs or plastic pouches in the produce section or Asian aisle of the supermarket.

1. Combine bonito flakes and broth in medium saucepan. Bring to a boil. Strain out bonito, reserving broth.

2. Heat oil in medium saucepan. Add leek and cook over medium heat 2 to 3 minutes or until tender, stirring frequently. Return broth to saucepan. Add miso; stir well. Add tofu and cook over low heat until heated through. *Makes 4 servings*

 Tip Miso soup is a standard breakfast item in Japan and has many health-giving properties attributed to it. Miso is a fermented product and the Japanese consider making miso an art comparable to cheese making in the Western world. The flavor of miso is rich, meaty and savory.

vietnamese beef soup

¾ pound boneless beef top sirloin or top round steak

6 cups beef broth

3 cups water

2 tablespoons minced fresh ginger

2 tablespoons soy sauce

1 cinnamon stick (3 inches long)

4 ounces rice noodles (rice sticks)

½ cup matchstick-size carrots

2 cups fresh bean sprouts

1 red onion, halved and thinly sliced

½ cup chopped fresh cilantro

½ cup chopped fresh basil

2 minced jalapeño peppers* *or* 1 to 3 teaspoons chili garlic sauce

*Jalapeño peppers can sting and irritate the skin, so wear rubber gloves when handling peppers and do not touch your eyes.

80

1. Freeze beef 45 minutes or until firm.

2. Meanwhile, combine broth, water, ginger, soy sauce and cinnamon stick in large saucepan. Bring to a boil over high heat. Reduce heat to low; cover and simmer 20 minutes. Remove and discard cinnamon stick.

3. Place rice noodles in large bowl. Cover with hot water; let stand 20 minutes or until softened. Drain.

4. Slice beef lengthwise in half, then crosswise into very thin strips. Add noodles and carrots to simmering broth; cook 2 to 3 minutes or until carrots are tender. Add beef and bean sprouts; cook 1 minute or until beef is no longer pink.

5. Remove from heat; stir in onion, cilantro, basil and jalapeño peppers.

Makes 6 servings

Noodles & Rice

Take a trip to an Asian market for an eye-opening look at the many kinds of noodles and rice available. So many delicious choices! Noodles can be crisp or slippery. Rice can be short-grain, long-grain, sushi-style or scented with jasmine.

soba stir-fry

8 ounces uncooked soba (buckwheat) noodles

1 tablespoon vegetable oil

2 cups sliced shiitake mushrooms

1 medium red bell pepper, cut into thin strips

2 whole dried red chiles *or* ¼ teaspoon red pepper flakes

1 clove garlic, minced

2 cups shredded napa cabbage

½ cup vegetable broth

2 tablespoons tamari or soy sauce

1 tablespoon rice wine or dry sherry

2 teaspoons cornstarch

1 package (14 ounces) firm tofu, drained and cut into 1-inch cubes

2 green onions, thinly sliced

1. Cook noodles according to package directions; drain.

2. Heat oil in wok or large nonstick skillet over medium heat. Add mushrooms, bell pepper, dried chiles and garlic. Cook and stir 3 minutes or until mushrooms are tender. Add cabbage. Cover; cook 2 minutes or until cabbage is wilted.

3. Combine broth, tamari, rice wine and cornstarch in small bowl. Stir into vegetable mixture. Cook 2 minutes or until sauce is thickened.

4. Stir in tofu and noodles; toss gently until heated through. Sprinkle with green onions. Serve immediately.

Makes 4 servings

donburi (beef & rice bowl)

1 cup uncooked short or medium grain white rice
3 teaspoons peanut or vegetable oil, divided
3 eggs, beaten
2 cups broccoli florets
1 small yellow onion, cut into thin wedges
1 pound boneless beef top sirloin steak, cut crosswise into thin strips
2 teaspoons cornstarch
¼ cup beef or chicken broth
3 tablespoons tamari or soy sauce
2 teaspoons dark sesame oil
¼ teaspoon red pepper flakes
¼ cup chopped fresh cilantro
¼ cup chopped green onions

1. Cook rice according to package directions.

2. Meanwhile, heat 1 teaspoon peanut oil in medium skillet over medium heat. Add eggs; cook 2 minutes or until bottom of omelet is set. Turn and cook 1 minute. Slide onto cutting board; let cool. Roll up omelet and cut crosswise into thin slices.

3. Heat 1 teaspoon peanut oil in same skillet; add broccoli and onion. Cook 4 to 5 minutes, stirring occasionally; remove from skillet. Combine beef strips and cornstarch in medium bowl. Heat remaining 1 teaspoon peanut oil in same skillet; stir-fry beef 2 minutes. Add broth, tamari, sesame oil and red pepper flakes. Simmer 2 minutes or until sauce thickens.

4. Stir sliced omelet, reserved vegetables, cilantro and green onions into skillet. Stir-fry 1 minute or until heated through. Serve over rice.   *Makes 4 servings*

lemon-ginger chicken with puffed rice noodles

Vegetable oil for frying

4 ounces thin rice noodles, broken in half

3 boneless skinless chicken breasts, cut into bite-size pieces

1 stalk lemongrass, cut into 1-inch pieces*

3 cloves garlic, minced

1 teaspoon minced fresh ginger

¼ teaspoon ground red pepper

¼ teaspoon black pepper

¼ cup water

1 tablespoon cornstarch

2 tablespoons peanut oil

6 ounces snow peas, trimmed

1 can (8¾ ounces) baby corn, rinsed and drained

¼ cup chopped fresh cilantro

2 tablespoons packed brown sugar

2 tablespoons fish sauce

1 tablespoon soy sauce

*Or substitute 1½ teaspoons grated lemon peel.

1. Heat 3 inches vegetable oil in wok or Dutch oven until oil registers 375°F on deep-fry thermometer. Fry noodles in small batches 20 seconds or until puffy, holding down noodles in oil with slotted spoon to fry evenly. Drain on paper towels; set aside.

2. Combine chicken, lemongrass, garlic, ginger, red pepper and black pepper in medium bowl. Combine water and cornstarch in small bowl; set aside.

3. Heat peanut oil in wok over high heat 1 minute. Add chicken mixture; stir-fry 3 minutes or until cooked through.

4. Add snow peas and baby corn; stir-fry 1 to 2 minutes. Stir cornstarch mixture; add to wok. Cook 1 minute or until thickened.

5. Add cilantro, brown sugar, fish sauce and soy sauce; cook until heated through. Discard lemongrass. Serve over rice noodles. *Makes 4 servings*

thai fried rice

2½ cups water

1⅓ cups long-grain white rice

½ pound ground pork or pork sausage

1 tablespoon vegetable oil

1 medium onion, thinly sliced

1 tablespoon minced fresh ginger

1 jalapeño pepper,* seeded and finely chopped

3 cloves garlic, minced

½ teaspoon ground turmeric or paprika

2 tablespoons fish sauce

2 cups chopped cooked vegetables such as broccoli, zucchini, red bell peppers, carrots, bok choy or spinach

3 eggs, lightly beaten

3 green onions, thinly sliced

½ cup cilantro leaves

Jalapeño peppers can sting and irritate the skin, so wear rubber gloves when handling peppers and do not touch your eyes.

1. Bring water and rice to a boil in medium saucepan over high heat. Reduce heat to low; cover and simmer 20 minutes or until water is absorbed.

2. Fluff rice with fork. Let cool to room temperature. Cover and refrigerate until cold, at least 1 hour or up to 24 hours.

3. Cook and stir pork in wok or medium skillet over medium-high heat until no longer pink. Drain fat. Transfer pork to bowl.

4. Heat oil in wok or large skillet over medium-high heat. Add onion, ginger, jalapeño, garlic and turmeric; stir-fry 4 to 6 minutes or until onion is tender.

5. Stir in fish sauce; mix well. Stir in cold rice, vegetables and pork; cook and stir 3 to 4 minutes or until heated through.

6. Push rice mixture to side of wok and pour eggs into center. Cook eggs 2 to 3 minutes or just until set, lifting and stirring to scramble. Stir rice mixture into eggs.

7. Stir in green onions. Transfer to serving bowl; sprinkle with cilantro.

Makes 4 servings

87

moo goo gai pan

1 package (about 1 ounce) dried shiitake mushrooms
¼ cup soy sauce
2 tablespoons rice vinegar
3 cloves garlic, minced
1 pound boneless skinless chicken breasts
½ cup chicken broth
1 tablespoon cornstarch
2 tablespoons peanut or vegetable oil, divided
1 can (about 7 ounces) straw mushrooms, rinsed and drained
3 green onions, cut into 1-inch pieces
   Hot cooked Chinese egg noodles or rice

1. Place dried mushrooms in small bowl; cover with hot water. Let stand 30 minutes or until softened. Drain; squeeze out excess water. Discard stems; slice caps.

2. Combine soy sauce, vinegar and garlic in medium bowl. Cut chicken crosswise into ½-inch strips. Add to soy sauce mixture; toss to coat. Marinate 20 minutes at room temperature. Blend broth and cornstarch in small bowl until smooth.

3. Heat 1 tablespoon oil in wok or large skillet over medium-high heat. Drain chicken, reserving marinade. Add chicken to wok; stir-fry 3 minutes or until cooked through. Remove to shallow dish. Heat remaining 1 tablespoon oil in wok. Add dried mushrooms, straw mushrooms and green onions; stir-fry 1 minute.

4. Stir cornstarch mixture; add to wok with reserved marinade. Bring to a boil; boil until sauce thickens. Return chicken along with any accumulated juices to wok; cook and stir until heated through. Serve over noodles. *Makes 4 servings*

three-topped rice

2½ cups uncooked short-grain rice
4¼ cups water, divided
  1 teaspoon salt, divided
1½ cups fresh or frozen green peas
  1 piece fresh ginger (about 1-inch square), grated
  2 tablespoons sugar, divided
  2 tablespoons sake or dry sherry, divided
  1 tablespoon plus 1 teaspoon soy sauce, divided
  ½ pound ground chicken
  4 eggs, lightly beaten
  1 ounce pickled ginger slices (optional)

1. Rinse and drain rice. Place in large saucepan. Add 2¾ cups water; soak 30 minutes. Stir in ½ teaspoon salt. Bring to a boil over medium-high heat. Reduce heat to low; cover and simmer 15 minutes or until liquid is absorbed. *Do not lift lid during cooking.* Remove from heat; let stand, covered, 15 minutes. Fluff rice; lay dry kitchen towel over saucepan; cover towel with lid. Let stand 10 minutes to absorb excess moisture.

2. Place peas, remaining 1½ cups water and ½ teaspoon salt in small saucepan. Bring to a boil over medium-high heat; boil 4 minutes or until peas are tender. Drain well. Squeeze enough fresh ginger to measure 1 teaspoon ginger juice into small cup. Combine 1 tablespoon sugar, 1 tablespoon sake, 1 tablespoon soy sauce and ginger juice in medium saucepan; bring to a boil over high heat. Add chicken; cook and stir 3 to 4 minutes or until chicken is no longer pink. Remove from heat.

3. Place eggs, remaining 1 tablespoon sugar, 1 tablespoon sake and 1 teaspoon soy sauce in medium skillet. Cook over medium-low heat 3 to 5 minutes or until eggs are set but still moist, stirring constantly. Remove from heat.

4. Divide rice among four individual serving bowls. Place equal amounts of chicken, eggs and peas over rice. Garnish with pickled ginger slices. *Makes 4 servings*

vegetarian sushi

1¼ cups Japanese short grain
    sushi rice*

1½ cups water

1 teaspoon dark sesame oil

4 medium shiitake mushrooms,
    sliced thin

½ red bell pepper

½ seedless cucumber

4 thin asparagus spears

2½ tablespoons seasoned rice vinegar

3 sheets nori

Prepared wasabi

Pickled ginger, soy sauce and
    additional prepared wasabi

If you can't find white rice labeled "sushi rice," use any short grain rice.

1. Rinse rice in several changes of water to remove excess starch; drain. Place in medium saucepan with 1½ cups water. Cover and bring to a boil. Reduce heat to very low. Cover; cook 15 to 20 minutes until rice is tender and liquid is absorbed. Let stand 10 minutes, covered.

2. Meanwhile, prepare fillings. Heat sesame oil in small nonstick skillet over medium heat. Cook and stir mushrooms 2 to 3 minutes or until tender. Slice bell pepper into very thin, long pieces. Cut cucumber into thin, long slivers, leaving skin on for color. Wrap asparagus in plastic wrap and microwave 1 minute to blanch.

3. Spoon warm rice into shallow nonmetallic bowl. Sprinkle vinegar over rice and fold in gently with wooden spoon. Cut sheet of nori in half lengthwise, parallel to lines marked on rough side. Place lengthwise, shiny side down, on bamboo rolling mat about 3 slats from edge nearest to you.

4. Prepare small bowl with water and splash of vinegar to rinse fingers and prevent rice from sticking while working. Spread about ½ cup rice over nori, leaving ½-inch border at top edge. Spread pinch of wasabi across center of rice. Arrange strips of two vegetables over wasabi.

5. Pick up edge of mat nearest you. Roll mat forward, wrapping rice around fillings and

pressing gently to form log. Once roll is formed, press gently to seal; place completed roll on cutting board, seam side down. Repeat with remaining nori, rice and fillings.

6. Slice each roll into 6 pieces with sharp knife. Wipe knife with damp cloth between cuts. Arrange sushi on serving plates with pickled ginger, soy sauce and additional wasabi for dipping.

Makes 6 sushi rolls (36 pieces)

asian noodle skillet

4 ounces soba (buckwheat) noodles
2 tablespoons vegetable oil, divided
1 pound firm tofu, cut into 1-inch cubes
4 cloves garlic, minced
1 tablespoon minced fresh ginger
1 can (8 ounces) water chestnuts
1 cup baby corn
1½ cups vegetable broth
1 cup snow peas
2 tablespoons soy sauce
¼ cup green onions, thinly sliced

1. Bring about 6 cups water to boil in large saucepan. Add noodles. Boil 1 minute or until softened. Rinse under cold water and drain.

2. Heat 1 tablespoon oil in large nonstick skillet over medium-high heat. Add tofu. Brown tofu on all sides. Remove to plate. Add remaining 1 tablespoon oil to skillet. Add garlic and ginger. Cook and stir about 1 minute or until fragrant. Stir in water chestnuts and corn.

3. Return browned tofu to skillet. Add broth, snow peas, soy sauce and drained noodles. Bring to boil. Reduce heat; simmer 3 minutes or until noodles are cooked through and most of liquid has evaporated. Stir in green onions. *Makes 4 servings*

lo mein noodles with shrimp

12 ounces thin Chinese wheat noodles (mein)
2 teaspoons dark sesame oil
1½ tablespoons oyster sauce
1½ tablespoons soy sauce
½ teaspoon sugar
¼ teaspoon salt
¼ teaspoon white or black pepper
2 tablespoons vegetable oil
1 teaspoon minced fresh ginger
1 clove garlic, minced
½ pound medium raw shrimp, peeled and deveined
1 bunch chives, cut into 1-inch pieces
1 tablespoon rice wine or dry sherry
8 ounces bean sprouts

94

1. Cook noodles according to package directions; drain and rinse under cold running water.

2. Combine noodles and sesame oil in large bowl; toss to coat. Combine oyster sauce, soy sauce, sugar, salt and pepper in small bowl.

3. Heat vegetable oil in wok or large skillet over high heat. Add ginger and garlic; stir-fry 10 seconds. Add shrimp; stir-fry 1 minute or until shrimp are pink and opaque. Add chives and wine; stir-fry until chives begin to wilt. Add half of bean sprouts; stir-fry 15 seconds. Add remaining bean sprouts; stir-fry 15 seconds.

4. Add oyster sauce mixture and noodles. Cook and stir 2 minutes or until heated through.

Makes 4 servings

sizzling rice cakes with mushrooms and bell peppers

¾ cup short grain rice*

1¾ cups water, divided

1 can (about 14 ounces) vegetable broth

1 tablespoon soy sauce

2 teaspoons sugar

2 teaspoons red wine vinegar

2 tablespoons cornstarch

3 tablespoons peanut oil, divided

1½ teaspoons minced fresh ginger

2 cloves garlic, thinly sliced

1 red bell pepper, cut into short strips

1 green bell pepper, cut into short strips

8 ounces button mushrooms, quartered

4 ounces fresh shiitake mushrooms, sliced

1 teaspoon dark sesame oil

Vegetable oil for frying

*Short grain rice works best in this recipe because of its sticky texture when cooked. It may be labeled sweet or glutinous rice.

1. Rinse rice under cold running water to remove excess starch. Combine rice and 1½ cups water in medium saucepan. Bring to a boil over medium-high heat. Reduce heat to low; cover and simmer 15 to 20 minutes or until liquid is absorbed. Let cool.

2. Combine broth, soy sauce, sugar and vinegar in medium bowl. Stir cornstarch into remaining ¼ cup water in small cup until smooth.

3. Heat 1 tablespoon peanut oil in wok or large skillet over medium-high heat. Add ginger and garlic; stir-fry 10 seconds. Add bell pepper strips; stir-fry 2 to 3 minutes or until crisp-tender. Remove and set aside.

4. Add remaining 2 tablespoons peanut oil to wok. Add mushrooms; stir-fry 2 to 3 minutes or until softened. Remove and set aside.

5. Add broth mixture to wok and bring to a boil. Stir cornstarch mixture; add to wok. Cook and stir until sauce boils and thickens slightly. Stir in sesame oil; return vegetables to wok. Remove from heat; cover to keep warm.

6. Shape rice into 12 cakes. (Wet hands to make handling rice easier.)

7. Heat 2 to 3 inches vegetable oil in large skillet over medium-high heat until oil registers 375°F on deep-fry thermometer. Add 4 rice cakes; cook 2 to 3 minutes or until puffed and golden, turning once. Drain on paper towels. Repeat with remaining rice cakes, reheating oil between batches.

8. Place rice cakes in serving bowl. Stir vegetable mixture; pour over rice cakes.

Makes 4 to 6 servings

udon noodles with chicken & spinach

3 tablespoons vegetable oil, divided
4 boneless skinless chicken thighs, cut into bite-size pieces
2 to 3 teaspoons grated fresh ginger
2 cloves garlic, minced
1 cup chicken broth
6 cups (6 ounces) coarsely chopped baby spinach
2 green onions, chopped
1 package (8 ounces) udon noodles, cooked and drained
1 tablespoon soy sauce

1. Heat 2 tablespoons oil in large nonstick skillet over medium heat. Add chicken and cook 4 to 6 minutes or until cooked through. Drain on paper towels.

2. Add remaining 1 tablespoon oil to skillet. Add ginger and garlic; cook over low heat 20 seconds or until garlic begins to color. Add broth; bring to a simmer.

3. Stir in spinach and green onions. Cook 2 to 3 minutes or until spinach wilts. Stir chicken and noodles into spinach mixture. Season with soy sauce. Serve immediately.

Makes 4 to 6 servings

97

pad thai

8 ounces uncooked rice noodles

2 tablespoons rice wine vinegar

1½ tablespoons fish sauce

1 to 2 tablespoons fresh lemon juice

1 tablespoon ketchup

2 teaspoons sugar

¼ teaspoon red pepper flakes

1 tablespoon vegetable oil

1 boneless skinless chicken breast, finely chopped

2 green onions, thinly sliced

2 cloves garlic, minced

3 ounces small raw shrimp, peeled, tails on

2 cups bean sprouts

¾ cup shredded red cabbage

1 medium carrot, shredded

3 tablespoons minced fresh cilantro

2 tablespoons chopped unsalted roasted peanuts

Lime wedges

1. Place noodles in medium bowl. Cover with warm water; let stand 30 minutes or until soft. Drain and set aside. Combine rice wine vinegar, fish sauce, lemon juice, ketchup, sugar and red pepper flakes in small bowl.

2. Heat oil in wok or large nonstick skillet over medium-high heat. Add chicken, green onions and garlic. Cook and stir until chicken is no longer pink. Stir in noodles; cook 1 minute. Add shrimp; cook about 3 minutes or until pink and opaque. Stir in fish sauce mixture; toss to coat evenly. Add bean sprouts and cook 2 minutes or until heated through.

3. Serve with shredded cabbage, carrot, cilantro, peanuts and lime wedges.

Makes 5 servings

vegetable lo mein with egg pancake

8 ounces uncooked thin Chinese wheat noodles (mein)

2 egg whites

1 egg

1 green onion, thinly sliced

Nonstick cooking spray

1 tablespoon dark sesame oil

2 cups thinly sliced bok choy

4 ounces shiitake mushrooms, tough stems discarded, caps sliced

1 small red or yellow bell pepper, cut into strips

½ cup vegetable broth

¼ cup teriyaki sauce

Chopped peanuts

Chopped cilantro

100

1. Cook noodles according to package directions; drain.

2. Meanwhile, beat egg whites and egg in small bowl until frothy. Stir in green onion. Spray large nonstick skillet with cooking spray; heat over medium heat. Add egg mixture; cook without stirring 2 to 3 minutes or until set on bottom. Carefully flip egg pancake; cook 1 minute or until set. Transfer to cutting board.

3. Heat sesame oil in same skillet over medium-high heat. Add bok choy, mushrooms and bell pepper; cook 4 to 5 minutes or until vegetables are tender. Add broth and teriyaki sauce; simmer 2 minutes.

4. Add vegetables to noodles; toss well. Cut egg pancake into strips. Gently toss with noodle mixture. Sprinkle with peanuts and cilantro. *Makes 4 servings*

 Tip The Chinese word for wheat noodles is "mein" or "mian." "Lo mein" simply means tossed noodles. The same mein noodles are used to make chow mein, but in that case they are fried to make them crisp.

korean-style beef & pasta

1 beef top round steak
(about ¾ pound)
2 tablespoons soy sauce
1 tablespoon rice wine or
dry sherry
2 teaspoons sugar
Korean-Style Dressing (page 103)
1 package (about 6 ounces)
medium rice noodles
2 cups thinly sliced napa cabbage
1¾ cups thinly sliced red and yellow
bell peppers
1 medium carrot, shredded
2 green onions, thinly sliced

1. Freeze beef until partially firm; cut into very thin slices.

2. Combine soy sauce, wine and sugar in small nonmetallic bowl. Add beef slices; toss to coat evenly. Cover and refrigerate 8 hours or overnight.

3. Remove beef from marinade; discard marinade. Prepare grill for direct cooking. Grill beef over medium-hot coals 2 to 3 minutes or until desired doneness.

4. Prepare Korean-Style Dressing.

5. Cook noodles in boiling water 1 to 2 minutes or until tender; drain and rinse under cold water. Arrange noodles on serving platter.

6. Combine cabbage, bell peppers, carrot, green onions and beef in medium bowl. Add Korean-Style Dressing; toss to coat evenly. Serve over noodles.   *Makes 6 to 8 servings*

korean-style dressing

2 teaspoons sesame seeds
⅓ cup orange juice
2 tablespoons rice wine or dry sherry
2 teaspoons soy sauce
1 teaspoon sugar
1 teaspoon grated fresh ginger
1 teaspoon dark sesame oil
1 clove garlic, minced
⅛ teaspoon red pepper flakes

1. Place sesame seeds in small nonstick skillet. Cook and stir over medium heat 3 minutes or until lightly browned and toasted. Cool completely.

2. Crush sesame seeds using mortar and pestle or wooden spoon; transfer to small bowl. Add orange juice, wine, soy sauce, sugar, ginger, sesame oil, garlic and red pepper flakes; blend well.

Makes about ½ cup

103

 Tip Rice wine is a slightly sweet wine made from fermented glutinous rice. Shaoxing rice wine is a good variety. Avoid those labeled "cooking wine," since they often have added salt or sugar. Dry sherry is an acceptable substitute.

bean threads with tofu and vegetables

8 ounces firm tofu, drained and cubed

1 tablespoon dark sesame oil

3 teaspoons soy sauce, divided

1 can (about 14 ounces) reduced-sodium chicken broth

1 package (3¾ ounces) uncooked bean thread noodles (see Tip)

1 package (16 ounces) frozen mixed vegetable medley such as broccoli, carrots and water chestnuts, thawed

¼ cup rice wine vinegar

½ teaspoon red pepper flakes

1. Place tofu on shallow plate; drizzle with sesame oil and 1½ teaspoons soy sauce.

2. Combine broth and remaining 1½ teaspoons soy sauce in wok or large deep skillet. Bring to a boil over high heat; reduce heat. Add bean threads; simmer until noodles are softened, stirring occasionally to separate noodles.

3. Stir in vegetables and vinegar; cook and stir until heated through. Stir in tofu mixture and red pepper flakes; cook 1 minute or until heated through. *Makes 6 servings*

 Tip Bean thread noodles are also called cellophane noodles or glass noodles. They are clear, thin noodles sold in tangled bunches and are made of mung bean flour.

Hot & Spicy

There are so many ways to heat things up Asian style! Ingredients include chili pastes, dried hot chiles, Szechuan peppercorns, hot chili oil and more. Each one has a deliciously different flavor and degree of fire.

chilled shrimp in chinese mustard sauce

1 cup water
½ cup dry white wine
2 tablespoons soy sauce
½ teaspoon Szechuan peppercorns or whole black peppercorns
1 pound large raw shrimp, peeled and deveined
¼ cup prepared sweet and sour sauce
2 teaspoons hot Chinese mustard

1. Combine water, wine, soy sauce and peppercorns in medium saucepan. Bring to a boil over high heat. Add shrimp; reduce heat to medium. Cover and simmer 2 to 3 minutes or until shrimp are pink and opaque. Drain well. Cover and refrigerate until chilled.

2. For mustard sauce, combine sweet and sour sauce and mustard in small bowl; mix well. Serve with shrimp. *Makes 6 servings*

Substitution: If you are unable to find hot Chinese mustard or simply want a sauce with less heat, substitute a brown or Dijon mustard.

Tip For this quick and easy recipe, the shrimp can be prepared up to one day in advance.

hunan chili beef

1 beef flank steak (about 1 pound)
3 tablespoons vegetable oil, divided
3 tablespoons soy sauce
1 tablespoon cornstarch
1 tablespoon rice wine or dry sherry
2 teaspoons brown sugar
1 cup drained canned baby corn
3 green onions, cut into 1-inch pieces
1 small piece fresh ginger, minced
2 cloves garlic, minced
¼ red bell pepper, cut into ¼-inch strips
1 jalapeño pepper,* cut into strips
1 teaspoon hot chili oil
Hot cooked rice

Jalapeño peppers can sting and irritate the skin, so wear rubber gloves when handling peppers and do not touch your eyes.

1. Cut flank steak lengthwise in half, then across the grain into ¼-inch-thick slices. Combine 1 tablespoon vegetable oil, soy sauce, cornstarch, wine and brown sugar in medium bowl. Add beef and toss to coat; set aside.

2. Heat 1 tablespoon oil in wok or large skillet over high heat 1 minute. Add half of beef mixture; stir-fry until well browned. Transfer to shallow dish. Repeat with remaining 1 tablespoon vegetable oil and beef mixture. Reduce heat to medium.

3. Add corn, green onions, ginger and garlic to wok; stir-fry 1 minute. Add bell pepper and jalapeño; stir-fry 1 minute.

4. Return beef and any accumulated juices to wok; add chili oil. Cook and stir until heated through. Serve with rice.

Makes 4 servings

spicy korean chicken wings

2 tablespoons peanut oil, plus additional for frying
2 tablespoons grated ginger
½ cup soy sauce
¼ cup cider vinegar
¼ cup honey
¼ cup chili garlic sauce
2 tablespoons orange juice
1 tablespoon dark sesame oil
18 chicken wings
    Sesame seeds (optional)

1. For sauce, heat peanut oil in medium skillet over medium-high heat. Add ginger; cook and stir 2 minutes. Add soy sauce, vinegar, honey, chili garlic sauce, orange juice and sesame oil; cook and stir 2 minutes. Remove from heat; set aside.

2. Heat 2 inches peanut oil in large heavy saucepan over medium-high heat until oil is 350° to 375°F; adjust heat to maintain temperature.

3. Remove and discard wing tips from chicken wings; pat dry.

4. Add chicken wings to oil in batches; cook 8 to 10 minutes or until crispy and brown and chicken is cooked through, turning once. Drain on paper towels.

5. Add wings to sauce; toss to coat. Sprinkle with sesame seeds.

Makes 6 to 8 servings

szechuan tuna steaks

4 tuna steaks (6 ounces each), cut 1 inch thick
¼ cup rice wine or sake
¼ cup soy sauce
1 tablespoon dark sesame oil
1 teaspoon hot chili oil *or* ¼ teaspoon red pepper flakes
1 clove garlic, minced
  Salad greens
3 tablespoons chopped fresh cilantro (optional)

1. Place tuna in single layer in large shallow glass dish. Combine sherry, soy sauce, sesame oil, hot chili oil and garlic in small bowl. Reserve ¼ cup soy sauce mixture. Pour remaining soy sauce mixture over tuna. Cover; marinate in refrigerator 40 minutes, turning once.

2. Spray grid with nonstick cooking spray. Prepare grill for direct cooking.

3. Drain tuna, discarding marinade. Grill tuna, uncovered, over medium-hot coals 6 minutes or until tuna is seared but still feels somewhat soft in center,* turning once. Transfer tuna to cutting board. Cut each tuna steak into thin slices. Serve with salad greens. Drizzle with reserved soy sauce mixture; sprinkle with cilantro.

Makes 4 servings

Tuna becomes dry and tough if overcooked. Cook to medium doneness for best results.

kung pao chicken

5 teaspoons rice wine or dry sherry, divided

5 teaspoons soy sauce, divided

3½ teaspoons cornstarch, divided

¼ teaspoon salt

1 pound boneless skinless chicken breasts, cut into bite-size pieces

2 tablespoons chicken broth or water

1 tablespoon red wine vinegar

1½ teaspoons sugar

3 tablespoons vegetable oil, divided

⅓ cup salted peanuts

6 to 8 small dried red chiles

1½ teaspoons minced fresh ginger

2 green onions, cut into 1½-inch pieces

1. For marinade, combine 2 teaspoons wine, 2 teaspoons soy sauce, 2 teaspoons cornstarch and salt in large bowl; mix well. Add chicken; stir to coat. Let stand 30 minutes.

2. Combine remaining 3 teaspoons wine, 3 teaspoons soy sauce, 1½ teaspoons cornstarch, broth, vinegar and sugar in small bowl.

3. Heat 1 tablespoon oil in wok or large skillet over medium heat. Add peanuts; stir-fry until lightly toasted. Remove and set aside. Heat remaining 2 tablespoons oil in wok over medium heat. Add chiles; stir-fry 1 minute or until chiles just begin to char.

4. Increase heat to high. Add chicken mixture; stir-fry 2 minutes. Add ginger; stir-fry 1 minute or until chicken is cooked though. Stir in peanuts and green onions. Stir cornstarch mixture; add to wok. Cook and stir until sauce boils and thickens.

Makes 3 servings

cellophane noodles with minced pork

1 package (about 4 ounces) cellophane noodles*
32 dried shiitake mushrooms
2 tablespoons minced fresh ginger
2 tablespoons black bean sauce
1½ cups chicken broth
1 tablespoon dry sherry
1 tablespoon soy sauce
2 tablespoons vegetable oil
½ pound ground pork
3 green onions, sliced
1 jalapeño or other hot pepper,** seeded and finely chopped
Cilantro sprigs and hot red peppers (optional)

*Cellophane noodles (also called bean threads or glass noodles) are thin, translucent noodles sold in tangled bunches.

**Jalapeño peppers can sting and irritate the skin, so wear rubber gloves when handling peppers and do not touch your eyes.

1. Place cellophane noodles and dried mushrooms in separate large bowls; cover each with hot water. Let stand 30 minutes; drain.

2. Cut cellophane noodles into 4-inch pieces. Squeeze out excess water from mushrooms. Cut off and discard mushroom stems; cut caps into thin slices.

3. Combine ginger and black bean sauce in small bowl. Combine broth, sherry and soy sauce in medium bowl.

4. Heat oil in wok or large skillet over high heat. Add pork; stir-fry 2 minutes or until no longer pink. Add green onions, jalapeño and black bean sauce mixture; stir-fry 1 minute.

5. Add broth mixture, noodles and mushrooms. Simmer 5 minutes or until most of liquid is absorbed. Garnish with cilantro and red peppers.   *Makes 4 servings*

spicy hunan ribs

1⅓ cups hoisin sauce or CATTLEMEN'S® Golden Honey Barbecue Sauce

⅔ cup FRANK'S® REDHOT® XTRA Hot Cayenne Pepper Sauce or
  FRANK'S® REDHOT® Cayenne Pepper Sauce

¼ cup soy sauce

2 tablespoons brown sugar

2 tablespoons dark sesame oil

2 tablespoons grated peeled ginger root

4 cloves garlic, crushed through a press

2 full racks pork spareribs, trimmed (about 6 pounds)

1. Combine hoisin sauce, XTRA Hot Sauce, soy sauce, brown sugar, sesame oil, ginger and garlic; mix well.

2. Place ribs into large resealable food storage bags. Pour 1½ cups sauce mixture over ribs. Seal bags and marinate in refrigerator 1 to 3 hours or overnight.

3. Prepare grill for indirect cooking over medium-low heat (250°F). Place ribs on rib rack or in foil pan; discard marinade. Cook on covered grill 2½ to 3 hours until very tender. Baste with remaining sauce during last 15 minutes of cooking. If desired, grill ribs over direct heat at end of cooking to char slightly.   *Makes 4 to 6 servings*

Prep Time: 5 minutes
Marinate Time: 1 hour
Cook Time: 3 hours

Tip Use Kansas City or St. Louis-style ribs for this recipe.

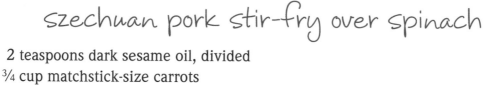

szechuan pork stir-fry over spinach

2 teaspoons dark sesame oil, divided
¾ cup matchstick-size carrots
½ pound pork tenderloin, cut into thin strips
3 cloves garlic, minced
2 teaspoons minced fresh ginger
¼ to ½ teaspoon red pepper flakes
1 tablespoon soy sauce
1 tablespoon mirin* or dry sherry
2 teaspoons cornstarch
8 ounces baby spinach
2 teaspoons sesame seeds, toasted**

Mirin, a sweet wine made from rice, is an essential flavoring in Japanese cuisine.

**To toast sesame seeds, spread in small skillet. Shake skillet over medium-low heat about 3 minutes or until seeds begin to pop and turn golden.*

1. Heat 1 teaspoon sesame oil in large nonstick skillet over medium-high heat. Add carrots. Stir-fry 3 minutes. Add pork, garlic, ginger and red pepper flakes. Stir-fry 3 minutes or until pork is barely pink in center.

2. Combine soy sauce, mirin and cornstarch in small bowl until well blended; add to pork mixture. Stir-fry about 1 minute or until sauce thickens.

3. Heat remaining 1 teaspoon oil in medium saucepan over medium-high heat. Add spinach. Cover and cook 1 minute or until spinach is barely wilted. Transfer spinach to two serving plates; top with pork mixture and sprinkle with sesame seeds.

Makes 2 servings

grilled swordfish with hot red sauce

2 tablespoons Sesame Salt (page 67)

4 swordfish or halibut steaks

¼ cup finely chopped green onions

2 tablespoons hot bean paste*

2 tablespoons soy sauce

4 teaspoons sugar

4 cloves garlic, minced

1 tablespoon dark sesame oil

⅛ teaspoon black pepper

*Also called chili bean paste or chili bean sauce.

1. Spray grid of grill or broiler rack with nonstick cooking spray. Prepare grill for direct cooking or preheat broiler.

2. Prepare Sesame Salt; set aside.

3. Rinse swordfish and pat dry with paper towels. Place in shallow glass dish.

4. Combine green onions, Sesame Salt, hot bean paste, soy sauce, sugar, garlic, sesame oil and pepper in small bowl; mix well.

5. Spread half of marinade over fish; turn and spread with remaining marinade. Cover with plastic wrap and refrigerate 30 minutes.

6. Remove fish from marinade; discard marinade. Place fish on prepared grid or broiler rack. Grill over medium heat or broil 8 to 10 minutes or until fish is opaque, turning once.

Makes 4 servings

szechuan eggplant

1 pound Asian eggplants
2 tablespoons peanut or vegetable oil
2 cloves garlic, minced
¼ teaspoon red pepper flakes *or* ½ teaspoon hot chili oil
¼ cup vegetable broth
¼ cup hoisin sauce
3 green onions, cut into 1-inch pieces
Toasted sesame seeds* (optional)

*To toast sesame seeds, spread in small skillet. Shake skillet over medium-low heat 3 minutes or until seeds begin to pop and turn golden.

1. Cut eggplants into ½-inch slices; cut each slice into ½×½-inch strips.

2. Heat peanut oil in wok or large nonstick skillet over medium-high heat. Add eggplant, garlic and red pepper flakes; stir-fry 7 minutes or until eggplant is very tender and browned.

3. Reduce heat to medium. Add broth, hoisin sauce and green onions to wok; cook and stir 2 minutes. Sprinkle with sesame seeds.   *Makes 4 to 6 servings*

 Tip Eggplants come in many shapes and sizes beyond the large purple Italian variety, which is the most common. Asian eggplants are slender and can be light purple, dark purple or a mix of the two. Since they have fewer and less developed seeds than larger varieties, they tend to be milder and less bitter. Their delicate skin does not need to be peeled.

spicy thai warm shrimp salad

¾ cup prepared vinaigrette salad dressing

⅓ cup chopped fresh mint leaves

¼ cup FRANK'S® REDHOT® XTRA Hot Sauce or FRANK'S® REDHOT® Cayenne Pepper Sauce

¼ cup FRENCH'S® Honey Dijon Mustard

1 tablespoon lime juice

1 tablespoon sucralose sugar substitute

1 tablespoon vegetable oil

1½ pounds large shrimp, shelled with tails left on

8 cups shredded napa cabbage

1 red bell pepper, thinly sliced

1 cup thinly sliced cucumber

1. Combine salad dressing, mint, XTRA Hot Sauce, mustard, lime juice and sugar substitute in large bowl; set aside.

2. Heat oil in large nonstick skillet or wok until hot. Stir-fry shrimp 2 to 3 minutes or until shrimp turn pink. Transfer to bowl with dressing. Add cabbage, bell pepper and cucumber; toss to coat. Serve warm. *Makes 6 servings*

Prep Time: 10 minutes
Cook Time: 5 minutes

szechuan grilled flank steak

1 beef flank steak (1¼ to 1½ pounds)
¼ cup seasoned rice wine vinegar
¼ cup soy sauce
2 tablespoons dark sesame oil
4 cloves garlic, minced
2 teaspoons minced fresh ginger
½ teaspoon red pepper flakes
¼ cup water
½ cup thinly sliced green onions
2 to 3 teaspoons sesame seeds, toasted*
    Hot cooked rice

To toast sesame seeds, spread in small skillet. Shake skillet over medium-low heat 3 minutes or until seeds begin to pop and turn golden.

1. Place steak in large resealable food storage bag. Combine vinegar, soy sauce, sesame oil, garlic, ginger and red pepper flakes in small bowl; pour over steak. Seal bag; turn to coat. Marinate in refrigerator 3 hours, turning once.

2. Prepare grill for direct cooking. Remove steak from bag, reserving marinade in small saucepan. Place steak on grid over medium heat. Grill, uncovered, 20 minutes for medium or until desired doneness, turning once.

3. Add water to reserved marinade. Bring to a rolling boil over high heat. Boil at least 1 minute. Slice steak across grain into thin slices. Drizzle slices with boiled marinade. Sprinkle with green onions and sesame seeds. Serve with rice. *Makes 4 to 6 servings*

Tofu & Such

Tofu just might be a miracle food. It can be enjoyed hot or cold, stir-fried, grilled or baked. It enhances flavor and adds protein to vegetarian dishes. Explore some delicious Asian ways to add tofu, seitan and tempeh to your meals.

sesame ginger-glazed tofu with rice

1 package (14 ounces) extra firm tofu
1 cup sesame ginger stir-fry sauce, divided
1 cup uncooked long grain rice
4 medium carrots, chopped (about 1 cup)
4 ounces snow peas, halved (about 1 cup)

1. To press tofu, cut in half horizontally. Cut each half into two triangles. Place tofu between layers of paper towels. Place flat, heavy object on top for 10 to 30 minutes.

2. Spread ½ cup stir-fry sauce in baking dish. Place tofu in sauce; marinate at room temperature 30 minutes, turning once.

3. Meanwhile, cook rice according to package directions. Keep warm.

4. Spray indoor grill pan with nonstick cooking spray; heat over medium-high heat. Grill tofu 6 to 8 minutes or until lightly browned, turning once.

5. Meanwhile, pour remaining ½ cup stir-fry sauce into large nonstick skillet; heat over medium-high heat. Add carrots and snow peas; cook and stir 4 to 6 minutes or until crisp-tender. Add rice; stir to combine.

6. Divide rice mixture between 4 plates; top each with tofu triangle.

Makes 4 servings

buddha's delight

1 package (1 ounce) dried shiitake mushrooms
1 package (about 12 ounces) firm tofu, drained
1 tablespoon peanut or vegetable oil
2 cups 1-inch asparagus pieces
1 medium onion, cut into thin wedges
2 cloves garlic, minced
½ cup vegetable broth
3 tablespoons hoisin sauce
¼ cup chopped fresh cilantro or thinly sliced green onions

1. Place mushrooms in small bowl; cover with hot water. Soak 30 minutes to soften. Drain over fine strainer, squeezing out excess water into measuring cup; reserve. Discard mushroom stems; slice caps.

2. Cut tofu in half horizontally; place between layers of paper towels. Place flat, heavy object on top for 10 to 30 minutes. Cut tofu into ¾-inch cubes or triangles.

3. Heat oil in wok or large skillet over medium-high heat. Add asparagus, onion and garlic; stir-fry 4 minutes.

4. Add mushrooms, ¼ cup reserved mushroom liquid, broth and hoisin sauce. Reduce heat to medium-low. Simmer 2 to 3 minutes or until asparagus is crisp-tender.

5. Stir in tofu until heated through. Sprinkle with cilantro.   *Makes 2 servings*

stir-fried eggplant and tofu

1 green onion
¼ pound ground pork
2 cloves garlic, minced
1 teaspoon minced fresh ginger
½ teaspoon dark sesame oil
4 ounces firm tofu
½ teaspoon cornstarch
½ cup chicken broth
1 pound Asian eggplants
2 tablespoons peanut oil
1 tablespoon soy sauce
1 teaspoon chili garlic sauce
½ teaspoon sugar

1. Mince white part of green onion. Cut green part of onion diagonally into 1½-inch lengths; reserve for garnish.

2. Combine pork, minced green onion, garlic, ginger and sesame oil in small bowl.

3. Drain tofu on paper towels. Cut into ½-inch cubes.

4. Stir cornstarch into broth in small bowl; set aside. Cut eggplant into 1-inch-thick pieces.

5. Heat peanut oil in wok or large skillet over high heat. Add eggplants; stir-fry 5 to 6 minutes or until tender. Add tofu; stir-fry 1 minute. Remove eggplant and tofu from wok; set aside.

6. Add pork mixture to wok; stir fry about 2 minutes or until browned. Add soy sauce, chili sauce and sugar; cook and stir until heated through.

7. Return eggplants and tofu to wok. Stir cornstarch mixture; add to wok. Cook and stir until sauce thickens.

Makes 4 servings

teriyaki tempeh with pineapple

1 package (8 ounces) unseasoned soy tempeh
1 cup island teriyaki sauce
1 cup uncooked rice
½ cup matchstick carrots
½ cup snow peas
½ cup matchstick-size red bell pepper strips
4 fresh pineapple rings

1. Heat 1 cup water in large deep skillet over high heat. Halve tempeh crosswise; add to skillet. Bring to a boil; reduce heat and boil gently 10 minutes. Drain water; add 1 cup teriyaki sauce to tempeh in skillet. Boil gently 10 minutes, turning tempeh occasionally. Drain and reserve teriyaki sauce in measuring cup; add additional sauce to make ½ cup.

2. Cook rice according to package directions. Heat reserved teriyaki sauce in wok or large nonstick skillet over medium-high heat. Add carrots, snow peas and bell pepper; cook and stir 4 to 6 minutes or until crisp-tender. Add rice; stir to combine. Add additional teriyaki sauce, if desired.

3. Prepare grill for direct cooking. Grill tempeh and pineapple rings over medium-high heat 10 minutes, turning once. Cut tempeh in half; serve over rice topped with pineapple. *Makes 4 servings*

Island Tempeh Sandwich: Omit rice and vegetables. Serve tempeh and pineapple on a soft roll with arugula, additional teriyaki sauce and mayonnaise, if desired.

 Tip Tempeh is a nutritious soy food that originated in Indonesia hundreds of years ago. It has a nutty, yeast flavor and chewy texture. You'll find it vacuum packed and refrigerated in natural food stores and some supermarkets.

rice noodles with broccoli and tofu

1 package (14 ounces) firm or extra firm tofu
1 package (8 to 10 ounces) wide rice noodles
2 tablespoons peanut oil
3 medium shallots, sliced
6 cloves garlic, minced
1 jalapeño pepper,* minced
2 teaspoons minced fresh ginger
3 cups broccoli florets
3 tablespoons regular soy sauce
1 tablespoon sweet soy sauce (or substitute regular)
1 to 2 tablespoons fish sauce
Fresh basil leaves (optional)

Jalapeño peppers can sting and irritate the skin, so wear rubber gloves when handling peppers and do not touch your eyes.

138

1. To press tofu, cut in half horizontally. Place tofu between layers of paper towels. Place flat, heavy object on top for 10 to 30 minutes. Place rice noodles in large bowl; cover with hot water. Soak 30 minutes or until softened.

2. Cut tofu into bite-size squares. Heat oil in wok or large skillet over medium-high heat. Add tofu; stir-fry 5 minutes or until lightly browned on all sides. Remove from skillet.

3. Add shallots, garlic, jalapeño pepper and ginger to skillet. Stir-fry 2 to 3 minutes. Add broccoli; stir-fry 1 minute. Cover and cook 3 minutes or until broccoli is crisp-tender.

4. Drain noodles; add to skillet and stir to combine. Return tofu to skillet; add soy sauces and fish sauce. Stir-fry 8 minutes or until noodles are coated and flavors are blended. Garnish with basil. *Makes 4 to 6 servings*

thai veggie curry

2 tablespoons vegetable oil

1 onion, quartered and thinly sliced

1 tablespoon Thai red curry paste (or to taste)

1 can (about 14 ounces) unsweetened coconut milk

2 red or yellow bell peppers, cut into strips

1½ cups cauliflower and broccoli florets

1 cup snow peas

1 package (about 14 ounces) tofu, pressed* and cubed

Salt and pepper

¼ cup slivered fresh basil

Hot cooked jasmine rice

*To press tofu, cut in half horizontally . Place tofu between layers of paper towels. Place flat, heavy object on top for 10 to 30 minutes.

1. Heat oil in wok or large skillet over medium-high heat. Add onion; cook and stir 2 minutes or until softened. Add curry paste; cook and stir to coat onion. Add coconut milk; bring to a boil, stirring to dissolve curry paste.

2. Add bell peppers, cauliflower and broccoli; simmer over medium heat 4 to 5 minutes or until crisp-tender. Stir in snow peas; simmer 2 minutes. Gently stir in tofu; cook until heated through. Season with salt and pepper. Sprinkle with basil; serve with rice.

Makes 4 to 6 servings

Tip Make sure to buy unsweetened coconut milk, which is usually sold in the Asian section of the supermarket. Other coconut products cannot be substituted. Coconut water is a beverage and cream of coconut (or coconut cream) is a sweetened product used for desserts and tropical drinks like piña coladas.

thai seitan stir-fry

1 package (8 ounces) seitan,* drained and thinly sliced

1 jalapeño pepper,** halved and seeded

3 cloves garlic

1 piece peeled fresh ginger

⅓ cup soy sauce

¼ cup packed brown sugar

¼ cup lime juice

½ teaspoon red pepper flakes

¼ teaspoon salt

3 tablespoons vegetable oil

1 medium onion, chopped (about 2 cups)

2 red bell peppers, quartered and thinly sliced (about 2 cups)

2 cups broccoli florets

3 green onions, sliced

4 cups lightly packed baby spinach

¼ cup shredded fresh basil

3 cups hot cooked rice

¼ cup salted peanuts, chopped

*Seitan is a meat substitute made from wheat gluten. It is high in protein and has a meaty, chewy texture. It can be found in the refrigerated section of large supermarkets and specialty food stores.

**Jalapeño peppers can sting and irritate the skin, so wear rubber gloves when handling and do not touch your eyes.

1. Place seitan slices in medium bowl. Combine jalapeño, garlic and ginger in food processor; process until finely chopped. Add soy sauce, brown sugar, lime juice, red pepper flakes and salt; process until blended. Pour mixture over seitan; toss to coat. Marinate at least 20 minutes at room temperature.

2. Heat oil in wok or large skillet over high heat. Add onion, bell peppers and broccoli. Stir-fry 3 to 5 minutes. Add seitan, marinade and green onions. Bring to a boil; stir-fry 3 minutes or until vegetables are crisp-tender and seitan is hot. Add spinach in batches, stirring until beginning to wilt after each addition.

3. Stir in basil just before serving. Serve over rice; sprinkle with peanuts.

Makes 4 to 6 servings

fried tofu with sesame dipping sauce

3 tablespoons soy sauce or tamari

2 tablespoons rice wine vinegar

2 teaspoons sugar

1 teaspoon sesame seeds, toasted*

1 teaspoon dark sesame oil

⅛ teaspoon red pepper flakes

1 package (14 ounces) extra firm tofu

2 tablespoons all-purpose flour

1 egg

¾ cup panko bread crumbs**

4 tablespoons vegetable oil

To toast sesame seeds, spread in small skillet. Shake skillet over medium-low heat about 3 minutes or until seeds begin to pop and turn golden.

**Panko bread crumbs are used in Japanese cooking to provide a crisp exterior to fried foods. They are coarser than ordinary bread crumbs.*

144

1. For dipping sauce, combine soy sauce, vinegar, sugar, sesame seeds, sesame oil and red pepper flakes in small bowl. Set aside.

2. Drain tofu and press between paper towels to remove excess water. Cut crosswise into 4 slices; cut each slice diagonally into triangles. Place flour in shallow dish. Beat egg in shallow bowl. Place panko in another shallow bowl.

3. Dip each piece of tofu in flour to lightly coat all sides; dip in egg, turning to coat. Drain; roll in panko to lightly coat.

4. Heat 2 tablespoons vegetable oil in large nonstick skillet over high heat. Reduce heat to medium; add half of tofu in single layer. Cook 1 to 2 minutes per side or until golden brown. Repeat with remaining oil and tofu. Serve with dipping sauce.

Makes 4 servings

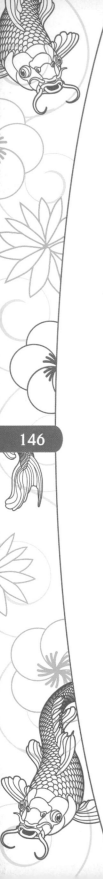

mongolian vegetables

1 package (14 ounces) firm tofu

4 tablespoons soy sauce, divided

1 tablespoon dark sesame oil

1 large head bok choy (about 1½ pounds)

2 teaspoons cornstarch

1 tablespoon peanut or vegetable oil

1 red or yellow bell pepper, cut into short thin strips

2 cloves garlic, minced

4 green onions, cut into ½-inch pieces

8 strips orange peel

2 teaspoons sesame seeds, toasted*

To toast sesame seeds, spread in small skillet. Shake skillet over medium-low heat 3 minutes or until seeds begin to pop and turn golden.

1. Press tofu lightly between paper towels to drain excess water; cut into ¾-inch squares. Place in shallow dish. Combine 2 tablespoons soy sauce and sesame oil in small bowl; drizzle over tofu. Let stand while preparing vegetables.

2. Cut stems from bok choy leaves; slice stems into ½-inch pieces. Cut leaves crosswise into ½-inch slices.

3. Blend remaining 2 tablespoons soy sauce into cornstarch in small bowl until smooth.

4. Heat peanut oil in wok or large skillet over medium-high heat. Add bok choy stems, bell pepper and garlic; stir-fry 5 minutes. Add bok choy leaves and green onions; stir-fry 2 minutes.

5. Stir cornstarch mixture and add to wok along with tofu mixture. Stir-fry 30 seconds or until sauce boils and thickens. Sprinkle with sesame seeds.   *Makes 2 servings*

spicy fried rice with tofu

4½ teaspoons vegetable oil, divided
2 eggs, lightly beaten
1 tablespoon minced garlic
1 tablespoon minced fresh ginger
½ teaspoon red pepper flakes
2 cups thinly sliced napa cabbage
1 cup chopped carrots
1 cup frozen green peas, thawed
3 cups cooked white rice
4 ounces firm tofu, drained and cut into ½-inch cubes
¼ cup vegetable broth
¼ cup soy sauce
3 tablespoons rice wine or dry sherry
2 teaspoons balsamic vinegar

148

1. Heat 1½ teaspoons oil in wok or large skillet over medium-high heat. Add eggs; cook and stir 2 to 3 minutes until set. Remove from wok; cut into small pieces. Set aside.

2. Heat remaining 3 teaspoons oil in same wok over high heat. Add garlic, ginger and red pepper flakes; cook 30 seconds or until fragrant. Add cabbage, carrots and peas; cook 5 to 10 minutes until carrots are crisp-tender.

3. Stir in rice, tofu, broth, soy sauce, wine and vinegar; cook and stir 3 minutes. Remove from heat. Stir in eggs.   *Makes 4 servings*

ma po tofu

1 package (14 ounces) firm tofu, drained and pressed*
2 tablespoons soy sauce
2 teaspoons minced fresh ginger
1 cup vegetable broth, divided
2 tablespoons black bean sauce
1 tablespoon cornstarch
1 tablespoon sweet chili sauce
2 tablespoons vegetable oil
1 green bell pepper, cut into bite-size pieces
2 cloves garlic, minced
1½ cups broccoli florets
¼ cup chopped fresh cilantro (optional)
   Hot cooked rice

*To press tofu, cut in half horizontally. Place tofu between layers of paper towels. Place flat, heavy object on top for 10 to 30 minutes.

1. Cut tofu into cubes. Place in shallow dish; sprinkle with soy sauce and ginger.

2. Combine ¼ cup broth, black bean sauce, cornstarch and chili sauce in small bowl; set aside.

3. Heat oil in wok or large skillet over high heat. Add bell pepper and garlic; cook and stir 2 minutes. Add remaining ¾ cup broth and broccoli. Bring to a boil; reduce heat, cover, and simmer 3 minutes or until broccoli is crisp-tender.

4. Stir sauce mixture and add to wok. Cook and stir 1 minute or until sauce boils and thickens. Stir in tofu and simmer, uncovered, until heated through. Sprinkle with cilantro. Serve with rice. *Makes 4 servings*

dragon tofu

1 package (14 ounces) firm tofu
¼ cup soy sauce
1 tablespoon creamy peanut butter
1 medium zucchini
1 medium yellow squash
1 medium red bell pepper
2 teaspoons peanut or vegetable oil
½ teaspoon hot chili oil
2 cloves garlic, minced
2 cups packed torn spinach
¼ cup coarsely chopped cashews or peanuts

1. Press tofu lightly between paper towels; cut into ¾-inch squares or triangles. Place in single layer in shallow dish. Whisk soy sauce into peanut butter in small bowl. Pour over tofu; stir gently to coat all surfaces. Let stand at room temperature 20 minutes.

2. Meanwhile, cut zucchini and yellow squash lengthwise into ¼-inch-thick slices; cut each slice into 2-inch strips. Slice bell pepper into 2-inch strips.

3. Heat peanut oil and chili oil in large skillet over medium-high heat. Add zucchini, yellow squash, bell pepper and garlic; stir-fry 3 minutes. Add tofu mixture; cook 2 minutes or until tofu is heated through and sauce is slightly thickened, stirring occasionally. Stir in spinach; remove from heat. Sprinkle with cashews before serving.

Makes 2 servings

Meat & Poultry

Asian cooks know how to get maximum flavor from even minimum amounts of meat. Explore Chinese stir-fries, Korean Beef Short Ribs or Japanese Fried Chicken to turn ordinary meal times into delectable adventures.

thai duck with beans and sprouts

    Juice of 1 lime (about 2 tablespoons)
2 tablespoons vegetable oil, divided
2 tablespoons soy sauce
1 tablespoon fish sauce
2 teaspoons minced fresh ginger
2 cloves garlic, minced
1 pound boneless skinless duck breast, cut into ¼-inch strips
1 cup chicken broth
1 tablespoon cornstarch
3 cups green beans
4 green onions, cut into 1-inch pieces
1½ cups bean sprouts

1. Combine lime juice, 1 tablespoon oil, soy sauce, fish sauce, ginger and garlic in medium bowl. Add duck; toss to coat well. Cover and refrigerate 30 minutes to 8 hours.

2. Whisk broth and cornstarch in small bowl; set aside.

3. Heat remaining 1 tablespoon oil in wok or large skillet over high heat. Remove duck from marinade; reserve marinade. Add duck to wok; stir-fry 4 minutes or until no longer pink. Remove duck from wok with slotted spoon.

4. Add green beans to skillet; stir-fry 5 to 6 minutes or until crisp-tender. Stir broth mixture. Add broth mixture, green onions and reserved marinade to skillet; boil 2 minutes. Return duck and accumulated juices to skillet and add bean sprouts. Cook and stir until heated through.

Makes 4 servings

fukien red-cooked pork

5¼ cups plus 3 tablespoons water, divided
2 pounds boneless pork shoulder, well trimmed, cut into 1½-inch chunks
⅓ cup rice wine or dry sherry
⅓ cup soy sauce
¼ cup lightly packed light brown sugar
1 piece fresh ginger (about 1½ inches), peeled and cut into strips
3 cloves garlic, chopped
1 teaspoon anise seeds
2 tablespoons cornstarch
1 pound carrots, sliced
½ head napa cabbage (about 1 pound), cut into 1-inch slices
1 teaspoon dark sesame oil

1. Place 4 cups water in wok or large skillet; bring to a boil over high heat. Add pork. Return to a boil; boil 2 minutes. Drain; return pork to wok. Add 1¼ cups water, wine, soy sauce, brown sugar, ginger, garlic and anise. Bring mixture to a boil. Cover; reduce heat to low and simmer 1¼ hours or until meat is almost tender, stirring occasionally.

2. Blend remaining 3 tablespoons water and cornstarch in cup until smooth; set aside.

3. Add carrots to wok; cover and cook 20 minutes or until pork and carrots are fork-tender. Transfer with slotted spoon to serving bowl.

4. Add cabbage to liquid in wok. Cover and increase heat to medium-high. Cook cabbage 2 minutes or until wilted. Stir cornstarch mixture until smooth; add to wok. Cook until sauce boils and thickens. Return pork and carrots to wok; add sesame oil and mix well.

Makes 4 to 5 servings

Note: "Red cooking" is a Chinese cooking method in which meat or poultry is braised in soy sauce, giving the meat a deep, rich color.

Sesame chicken

1 pound boneless skinless chicken breasts or thighs, cut into bite-size pieces
⅔ cup teriyaki sauce, divided
2 teaspoons cornstarch
1 tablespoon peanut oil
2 cloves garlic, minced
2 green onions, sliced
1 tablespoon sesame seeds, toasted*
1 teaspoon dark sesame oil

To toast sesame seeds, spread in small skillet. Shake skillet over medium-low heat about 3 minutes or until seeds begin to pop and turn golden.

1. Toss chicken with ⅓ cup teriyaki sauce in medium bowl. Marinate 15 to 20 minutes in refrigerator.

2. Drain chicken; discard marinade. Blend remaining ⅓ cup teriyaki sauce and cornstarch in small bowl until smooth.

3. Heat peanut oil in wok or large skillet over medium-high heat. Add chicken and garlic; stir-fry 3 minutes or until chicken is cooked through. Stir cornstarch mixture; add to wok. Cook and stir 1 minute or until sauce boils and thickens. Stir in green onions, sesame seeds and sesame oil. Serve immediately.   *Makes 4 servings*

Tip

Sesame seeds come in different colors depending on the variety, including brown, red, black and yellow. The most common is a pale ivory. You can purchase sesame seeds in the spice section at supermarkets, but Asian markets may have a better selection and lower prices. The seeds are quite perishable, so buy them someplace that has a high turnover and in small quantities that you will use quickly. Store them in an airtight container in a cool dry place. Better yet, refrigerate or freeze them.

cantonese tomato beef

1 beef flank steak, trimmed (about 1 pound)

2 tablespoons soy sauce

2 tablespoons dark sesame oil, divided

1 tablespoon plus 1 teaspoon cornstarch, divided

1 pound thin Chinese wheat noodles (mein)

1 cup beef broth

2 tablespoons brown sugar

1 tablespoon cider vinegar

2 tablespoons vegetable oil, divided

1 tablespoon minced fresh ginger

3 small onions, cut into wedges

2 pounds ripe tomatoes, cored and cut into wedges

1 green onion, thinly sliced

1. Cut flank steak lengthwise in half, then crosswise into ¼-inch-thick slices. Combine soy sauce, 1 tablespoon sesame oil and 1 teaspoon cornstarch in large bowl. Add beef slices; toss to coat. Marinate 30 minutes at room temperature.

2. Cook noodles according to package directions. Drain; toss with remaining 1 tablespoon sesame oil. Keep warm. Combine broth, brown sugar, remaining 1 tablespoon cornstarch and vinegar in small bowl; set aside.

3. Heat 1 tablespoon vegetable oil in wok or large skillet over high heat. Add beef mixture and stir-fry over high heat 5 minutes or until lightly browned. Transfer beef to shallow dish. Reduce heat to medium. Add ginger and stir-fry 30 seconds.

4. Heat remaining 1 tablespoon vegetable oil. Add onion wedges; cook and stir 2 minutes or until tender. Stir in half of tomato wedges. Stir broth mixture and add to wok. Cook and stir until liquid boils and thickens.

5. Return beef and any accumulated juices to wok. Add remaining tomato wedges; cook and stir until heated through. Serve over cooked noodles. Sprinkle with green onion.

Makes 4 servings

twice-fried chicken thighs with plum sauce

½ cup Plum Sauce (recipe follows)
1 cup peanut oil
1 to 1¼ pounds boneless skinless chicken thighs, cut into strips
4 medium carrots, cut into strips
4 green onions, sliced
½ teaspoon salt
½ teaspoon red pepper flakes
   Hot cooked rice
1 tablespoon sesame seeds, toasted*

*To toast sesame seeds, spread in small skillet. Shake skillet over medium-low heat about 3 minutes or until seeds begin to pop and turn golden.

1. Prepare Plum Sauce.

2. Heat oil in wok over high heat until oil registers 375°F on deep-fry thermometer. Place chicken in oil; fry 1 minute. Remove with slotted spoon; drain on paper towels. Drain oil from wok, reserving 2 tablespoons.

3. Add 1 tablespoon reserved oil to wok. Heat over high heat. Add carrots; stir-fry 5 minutes until crisp-tender. Remove from wok; set aside.

4. Add remaining 1 tablespoon oil to wok. Add chicken and green onions; stir-fry 1 minute. Stir in Plum Sauce, carrots, salt and red pepper flakes. Cook and stir 2 minutes. Serve over rice; top with sesame seeds.   *Makes 4 servings*

plum sauce

1 cup plum preserves
½ cup prepared chutney, chopped
2 tablespoons brown sugar
2 tablespoons lemon juice
2 cloves garlic, minced
2 teaspoons soy sauce
2 teaspoons minced fresh ginger

Combine all ingredients in small saucepan. Cook and stir over medium heat until preserves are melted.

Makes 1 cup

beef teriyaki stir-fry

1 cup uncooked rice
1 boneless beef top sirloin steak (about 1 pound)
½ cup teriyaki sauce
2 tablespoons vegetable oil, divided
1 medium onion, sliced
2 cups frozen green beans, thawed

1. Cook rice according to package directions. Keep warm.

2. Cut beef lengthwise in half, then crosswise into ⅛-inch slices. Combine beef and ¼ cup teriyaki sauce in medium bowl; set aside.

3. Heat 1½ teaspoons oil in wok or large skillet over medium-high heat. Add onion; stir-fry 3 to 4 minutes or until crisp-tender. Remove from skillet to another medium bowl.

4. Heat 1½ teaspoons oil in skillet. Stir-fry green beans 3 minutes or until crisp-tender and heated through. Drain excess liquid. Add beans to onion in bowl.

5. Heat remaining 1 tablespoon oil in skillet. Drain beef, discarding marinade. Stir-fry half of beef 2 minutes or until barely pink in center. Add to vegetables. Repeat with remaining beef. Return beef mixture to skillet. Stir in remaining ¼ cup teriyaki sauce; cook and stir 1 minute or until heated through. Serve with rice.

Makes 4 to 6 servings

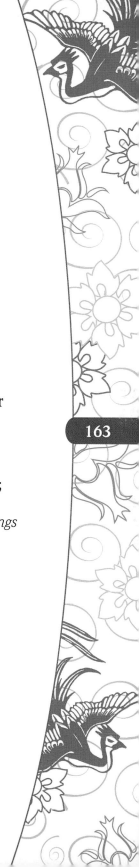

163

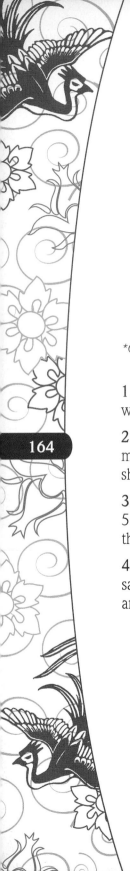

sweet and sour pork

1 tablespoon soy sauce

2 cloves garlic, minced

1 pound boneless pork loin or tenderloin*

1 can (8 ounces) pineapple chunks in juice, undrained

2 tablespoons peanut or vegetable oil, divided

2 medium carrots, sliced

1 large green bell pepper, cut into 1-inch pieces

⅓ cup stir-fry sauce

1 tablespoon white wine

Hot cooked rice

*Or substitute 1 pound boneless skinless chicken breasts or thighs.

1. Combine soy sauce and garlic in medium bowl. Cut pork into 1-inch pieces; toss with soy sauce mixture. Drain pineapple, reserving 2 tablespoons juice.

2. Heat 1 tablespoon oil in wok or large skillet over medium-high heat. Add pork mixture; stir-fry 4 to 5 minutes or until pork is barely pink in center. Transfer pork to shallow dish.

3. Heat remaining 1 tablespoon oil in wok. Add carrots and bell pepper; stir-fry 4 to 5 minutes or until vegetables are crisp-tender. Add pineapple; stir-fry until heated through.

4. Add stir-fry sauce, reserved pineapple juice and wine; stir-fry 30 seconds or until sauce comes to a boil. Return pork along with any accumulated juices to wok; cook and stir until heated through. Serve over rice.   *Makes 4 servings*

caramelized lemongrass chicken

2 stalks lemongrass

1½ pounds skinless chicken thighs (4 to 6 thighs)

¼ cup sugar

3 tablespoons fish sauce

2 cloves garlic, slivered

¼ teaspoon black pepper

1 tablespoon vegetable oil

1 tablespoon lemon juice

Hot cooked rice

Lemon slices

1. Remove outer leaves from lemongrass and discard. Trim off and discard upper stalks. Flatten lemongrass with meat mallet. Cut lemongrass into 1-inch pieces.

2. Place chicken in large resealable food storage bag; add sugar, fish sauce, garlic, pepper and lemongrass. Seal bag; turn to coat. Marinate in refrigerator at least 1 hour or up to 4 hours, turning occasionally.

3. Heat oil in large skillet over medium heat. Remove chicken from marinade; reserve marinade. Cook chicken 10 minutes or until browned, turning once.

4. Pour reserved marinade into skillet; bring to a boil. Boil 2 minutes. Reduce heat to low; cover and simmer 30 minutes or until chicken is cooked through, turning occasionally.

5. Stir lemon juice into skillet. Turn chicken to coat. Serve with rice and lemon slices.

Makes 4 servings

five-spice beef and bok choy

1 boneless beef top sirloin steak (about 1 pound)
¼ cup soy sauce
2 tablespoons rice wine or dry sherry
2 teaspoons minced fresh ginger
2 cloves garlic, minced
1 teaspoon sugar
½ teaspoon Chinese five-spice powder*
¼ teaspoon red pepper flakes (optional)
1 large head bok choy
2 teaspoons cornstarch
2 tablespoons peanut oil or vegetable oil, divided
Hot cooked rice

Chinese five-spice powder consists of cinnamon, cloves, fennel seed, star anise and Szechuan peppercorns.

1. Cut beef lengthwise in half, then crosswise into ⅛-inch-thick slices. Combine soy sauce, wine, ginger, garlic, sugar, five-spice powder and red pepper flakes, if desired, in medium bowl. Add beef and toss to coat; set aside.

2. Separate bok choy leaves from stems. Stack leaves and cut into 1-inch slices. Cut stems into ½-inch slices. Keep leaves and stems separate.

3. Drain beef, reserving marinade. Stir reserved marinade into cornstarch in small bowl; stir until smooth. Set aside.

4. Heat 1 tablespoon oil in wok or large skillet over medium-high heat. Add half of beef; stir-fry 2 minutes or until beef is barely pink in center. Transfer beef to shallow dish. Repeat with remaining beef.

5. Add remaining 1 tablespoon oil and heat 30 seconds. Add bok choy stems; stir-fry 3 minutes. Add bok choy leaves; stir-fry 2 minutes.

6. Stir marinade mixture until smooth; add to wok. Boil 1 minute or until sauce thickens.

7. Return beef and any accumulated juices to wok; cook until heated through. Serve over rice.
Makes 4 servings

teppanyaki

⅓ cup tamari or soy sauce

2 tablespoons mirin (Japanese sweet rice wine)

1 tablespoon lemon juice

1 tablespoon orange juice

⅛ to ¼ teaspoon red pepper flakes (optional)

4 small frozen corn on the cob, thawed

2 to 3 tablespoons vegetable oil

2 medium zucchini or yellow squash, cut into thin slices

4 ounces shiitake mushrooms, stemmed and cut into thick slices

½ pound beef tenderloin or top loin steak, thinly sliced crosswise

½ pound pork tenderloin, thinly sliced crosswise

½ pound medium raw shrimp, peeled and deveined

1. For dipping sauce, combine tamari, mirin, lemon juice, orange juice and red pepper flakes, if desired, in small bowl; set aside.

2. Heat oven to 225°F to keep food warm while cooking. Cook corn in microwave according to package directions just until heated through. Heat large cast iron grill pan or heavy skillet over medium-high heat. Brush with oil. Brown corn 2 minutes, turning frequently. Transfer to large baking pan; place in oven to keep warm.

3. Cook zucchini 2 to 3 minutes or until browned and tender, adding oil if needed. Transfer to oven to keep warm. Cook mushrooms 2 to 3 minutes or until tender; keep warm.

4. Cook beef slices 2 minutes or until browned and tender, adding more oil as needed; keep warm. Cook pork 3 minutes; keep warm. Cook shrimp 2 to 3 minutes or until pink and opaque, turning occasionally.

5. Arrange vegetables, meat and shrimp on warm serving plates. Serve with dipping sauce.   *Makes 4 servings*

Serving Suggestion: Teppanyaki is often served with several dipping sauces. A traditional ponzu sauce, as in this recipe, is usually one of them. If you'd like, create a ginger dipping sauce by adding minced fresh ginger, sake and a bit of wasabi to tamari or soy sauce.

korean beef short ribs

2½ pounds beef chuck flanken-style short ribs (see Tip)

¼ cup chopped green onions

¼ cup water

¼ cup soy sauce

1 tablespoon sugar

2 teaspoons grated fresh ginger

2 teaspoons dark sesame oil

2 cloves garlic, minced

½ teaspoon black pepper

1 tablespoon sesame seeds, toasted*

*To toast sesame seeds, spread in small skillet. Shake skillet over medium-low heat about 3 minutes or until seeds begin to pop and turn golden.

1. Place ribs in large resealable food storage bag. Combine green onions, water, soy sauce, sugar, ginger, sesame oil, garlic and pepper in small bowl; pour over ribs. Seal bag; turn to coat. Marinate in refrigerator at least 4 hours or up to 8 hours, turning occasionally.

2. Prepare grill for direct cooking over medium-high heat.

3. Drain ribs; reserve marinade. Grill, covered, 5 minutes. Brush tops lightly with reserved marinade; turn and brush again. Discard remaining marinade. Grill, covered, 5 to 6 minutes for medium or until desired doneness. Sprinkle with sesame seeds.

Makes 4 to 6 servings

 Tip Barbecued beef short ribs are a classic Korean dish called "kalbi." Look for Korean-style short ribs at an Asian market. The cut refers to a thin strip of beef 8 to 10 inches long, cut across the bone from the chuck end of the short ribs. Unlike American short ribs, which are thick and tough unless cooked long and slow, Korean style short ribs are cut lengthwise, resulting in a thin strip of meat that is ideal on the grill.

almond chicken

1½ cups water

4 tablespoons rice wine or dry sherry, divided

4½ teaspoons plus 1 tablespoon cornstarch, divided

4 teaspoons soy sauce

1 teaspoon chicken bouillon granules

1 egg white, beaten

½ teaspoon salt

2 pounds boneless skinless chicken breasts, cut into 1-inch pieces

Vegetable oil for frying

½ cup blanched whole almonds

1 large carrot, diced

1 teaspoon minced fresh ginger

6 green onions, cut into 1-inch pieces

3 stalks celery, cut into ½-inch pieces

8 fresh mushrooms, sliced

½ cup sliced bamboo shoots (½ of 8-ounce can), drained

1. Combine water, 2 tablespoons wine, 4½ teaspoons cornstarch, soy sauce and bouillon granules in small saucepan. Cook and stir over medium heat 5 minutes or until mixture boils and thickens. Keep warm.

2. Combine remaining 2 tablespoons wine, 1 tablespoon cornstarch, egg white and salt in medium bowl. Add chicken; stir to coat well.

3. Heat oil in wok or large skillet over high heat to 375°F. Add half of chicken; cook 3 to 5 minutes or until cooked through. Drain on paper towels. Repeat with remaining chicken.

4. Drain all but 2 tablespoons oil from wok. Add almonds; stir-fry 2 minutes or until golden. Transfer almonds to small bowl. Add carrot and ginger to wok; stir-fry 1 minute. Add green onions, celery, mushrooms and bamboo shoots; stir-fry 3 minutes or until crisp-tender. Stir in chicken, almonds and sauce; cook and stir until heated through.

Makes 4 to 6 servings

japanese fried chicken on watercress

1 pound boneless skinless chicken breasts, cut into 2-inch pieces
3 tablespoons tamari or soy sauce
2 tablespoons sake
3 cloves garlic, minced
1 teaspoon minced fresh ginger
  Peanut oil for deep frying
⅓ cup cornstarch
3 tablespoons all-purpose flour

Salad

¼ cup unseasoned rice vinegar
3 teaspoons tamari or soy sauce
1 teaspoon dark sesame oil
2 bunches watercress, trimmed of tough stems
1 pint grape tomatoes, halved

1. Place chicken in large resealable food storage bag. Mix 3 tablespoons tamari, sake, garlic and ginger in small bowl. Pour over chicken and marinate in refrigerator at least 30 minutes, turning occasionally.

2. Heat at least 1½ inches peanut oil to 350°F in deep heavy saucepan over medium-high heat. Combine cornstarch and flour in shallow dish. Remove chicken from marinade; discard marinade. Roll chicken in cornstarch mixture and shake off excess.

3. Deep fry chicken in batches 4 to 6 minutes or until golden and no longer pink in center. Do not crowd pan. Drain on paper towels.

4. For salad dressing, whisk vinegar, 3 teaspoons tamari and sesame oil in small bowl. Arrange watercress and tomatoes on serving plates. Drizzle with dressing and top with chicken.

Makes 4 servings

Fish & Seafood

Seafood is revered and treated with great care by Asian cooks. Share some of their simple but amazing methods with steamed fish, Thai Shrimp Curry and more. If you're fishing for culinary compliments, you'll find the recipes here.

miso salmon & spinach

- 1 cup sake
- ¼ cup white miso*
- ¼ cup mirin (Japanese sweet rice wine)
- 4 boneless skinless salmon fillets or steaks
- 1 bag (10 ounces) baby spinach
- Soy sauce
- 2 teaspoons white and black sesame seeds

Miso is a fermented soybean paste used frequently in Japanese cooking. Miso comes in many varieties; the light yellow miso, usually labeled "white" is the mildest. Look for it in tubs or plastic pouches in the produce section or Asian aisle of the supermarket.

1. Combine sake, miso and mirin in large deep skillet or Dutch oven. Bring to a boil over high heat. Reduce heat to medium; add salmon. Simmer 4 minutes. Turn salmon over; simmer 3 to 4 minutes or until center is opaque. Transfer salmon to plate and keep warm.

2. Add spinach to liquid in skillet in two batches; cook 2 minutes or until wilted. Remove with slotted spoon and keep warm.

3. Increase heat to high and bring liquid to a gentle boil. Cook 1 to 2 minutes or until sauce is reduced to about ¼ cup. Season with soy sauce.

4. Serve salmon over spinach; drizzle with sauce and sprinkle with sesame seeds.

Makes 4 servings

thai shrimp curry

1 can (about 14 ounces) unsweetened coconut milk, divided
1 teaspoon Thai red curry paste
⅓ cup water
1 tablespoon packed brown sugar
1 tablespoon fish sauce
  Peel of 1 lime, finely chopped
1 pound large raw shrimp, peeled and deveined
½ cup fresh basil leaves, thinly sliced
  Hot cooked jasmine rice
  Fresh pineapple wedges (optional)
½ cup unsalted peanuts (optional)

1. Pour half of coconut milk into large skillet. Bring to a boil over medium heat, stirring occasionally. Reduce heat to medium-low; simmer 5 to 6 minutes. Oil may start to rise to surface. Stir in curry paste. Cook and stir 2 minutes.

2. Combine remaining half of coconut milk and water in small bowl. Add to skillet with brown sugar, fish sauce and lime peel. Cook over medium-low heat 10 to 15 minutes or until sauce thickens slightly.

3. Add shrimp and basil; reduce heat to low. Cook 3 to 5 minutes or until shrimp are pink and opaque. Serve over rice; garnish with pineapple and peanuts.

Makes 4 servings

 Tip Jasmine rice is a long grain rice with a delightful aroma. It is also known as fragrant or scented rice and is named after the sweet smelling jasmine flower. It was first grown for the royalty of the kingdom of Siam. It cooks up soft, white and fluffy.

fish rolls with crab sauce

1 pound thin sole fillets
1 tablespoon rice wine or
   dry sherry
2 teaspoons dark sesame oil
1 green onion, finely chopped
1 teaspoon minced fresh ginger
½ teaspoon salt
   Dash white pepper

Crab Sauce

1½ tablespoons cornstarch
2 tablespoons water
1 tablespoon vegetable oil
1 teaspoon minced fresh ginger
6 ounces fresh crabmeat, flaked*
2 green onions, thinly sliced
1 tablespoon rice wine or
   dry sherry
1¼ cups chicken broth
¼ cup milk

Pick out and discard any shell or cartilage from crabmeat.

1. If fillets are large, cut in half crosswise (each piece should be 5 to 6 inches long). Combine 1 tablespoon wine, sesame oil, chopped green onion, 1 teaspoon ginger, salt and white pepper in small bowl. Brush each piece of fish with wine mixture; let stand 30 minutes.

2. Fold fillets into thirds; place on rimmed heatproof dish that will fit inside a steamer. Place dish on rack in steamer. Cover and steam 8 to 10 minutes over boiling water until fish turns opaque and begins to flake when tested with fork.

3. For Crab Sauce, blend cornstarch and water in small cup. Heat vegetable oil in medium saucepan over medium heat. Add 1 teaspoon ginger; cook and stir 10 seconds. Add crabmeat, sliced green onions and 1 tablespoon wine; stir-fry 1 minute. Add broth and milk; bring to a boil. Stir cornstarch mixture; add to saucepan. Cook until sauce boils and thickens slightly, stirring constantly.

4. Transfer fish to serving platter; top with Crab Sauce.   *Makes 4 to 6 servings*

beijing fillet of sole

2 tablespoons soy sauce

2 teaspoons dark sesame oil

4 sole fillets (about 6 ounces each)

1¼ cups shredded cabbage or coleslaw mix

½ cup crushed chow mein noodles

1 egg white, lightly beaten

2 teaspoons sesame seeds

1. Preheat oven to 350°F. Line shallow baking pan with foil. Combine soy sauce and sesame oil in small bowl. Place sole in shallow dish. Lightly brush both sides of sole with 1 tablespoon soy sauce mixture.

2. Combine cabbage, noodles, egg white and remaining soy sauce mixture in medium bowl. Spoon evenly in center of each fillet. Roll up fillets. Place seam side down in prepared pan. Sprinkle rolls with sesame seeds.

3. Bake 25 to 30 minutes or until fish begins to flake when tested with fork.

Makes 4 servings

183

scallop stir-fry with black bean and stout sauce

1 can (about 15 ounces) black beans, rinsed and drained

⅓ cup stout or dark beer

2 tablespoons soy sauce

2 tablespoons honey

2 teaspoons hoisin sauce

2 cloves garlic, minced

½ teaspoon salt

⅛ teaspoon red pepper flakes

2 tablespoons vegetable oil

1 red bell pepper, cut into thin strips

1½ cups snow peas

1½ cups thinly sliced carrots

1½ pounds sea scallops

1. Combine beans, stout, soy sauce, honey, hoisin sauce, garlic, salt and red pepper flakes in food processor or blender; process until combined.

2. Heat oil in large nonstick skillet over medium-high heat. Add bell pepper, snow peas and carrots; stir-fry 3 minutes. Add scallops and black bean sauce; stir-fry 6 minutes or until scallops are opaque and mixture is heated through.   *Makes 4 to 6 servings*

pressed sushi (oshizushi)

1½ cups short grain sushi rice

3 tablespoons seasoned rice vinegar

1 large red bell pepper

1 large yellow bell pepper

1 tablespoon tamari or soy sauce

1 tablespoon mirin (Japanese sweet rice wine)

¼ cup finely chopped unpeeled cucumber

4 ounces thinly sliced smoked salmon

   Salmon roe (caviar) and herb leaves (optional)

1. Prepare rice according to package directions. Spread warm rice in large wooden bowl or on parchment lined baking sheet. Sprinkle with vinegar and gently fold into rice with wooden spoon or spatula. Cover with damp clean cloth and set aside. *Do not refrigerate.*

2. Meanwhile, preheat broiler. Cut bell peppers lengthwise into quarters; place skin sides up on foil-lined baking sheet. Broil 3 to 4 inches from heat source 10 minutes or until skins are blackened. Wrap peppers in foil; let stand 10 minutes. Peel off and discard skins.

3. Line 8-inch square baking dish with foil, allowing foil to extend over edges of pan for easy removal. Spoon half of rice into prepared pan; press down firmly. Arrange pepper pieces over rice in single layer, covering rice completely. Combine tamari and mirin in small cup; drizzle over peppers.

4. Combine remaining half of rice and cucumber. Spoon evenly over peppers and press down firmly. Arrange salmon over rice, covering entire surface; press down firmly. Cover with plastic wrap. Place another 8-inch square baking dish on top of plastic; weigh down with heavy objects. Let stand at room temperature 1 hour or refrigerate up to 6 hours.

5. Remove weighted pan and plastic wrap. Use foil to transfer pressed sushi to cutting board. Cut into squares or rectangles. Garnish with salmon roe and herbs.

Makes 4 main dish or 8 side dish servings

crab-stuffed shrimp

Sauce

- 2 tablespoons vegetable oil
- 1 small yellow onion, finely chopped
- 1 teaspoon curry powder
- 1½ tablespoons rice wine or dry sherry
- 1 tablespoon satay sauce
- 2 teaspoons soy sauce
- 1 teaspoon sugar
- ¼ cup whipping cream or milk

Shrimp

- 2 egg whites, lightly beaten
- 4 teaspoons cornstarch
- 1 tablespoon rice wine or dry sherry
- 1 tablespoon soy sauce
- 2 cans (6½ ounces each) crabmeat, drained and flaked*
- 8 green onions, finely chopped
- 2 stalks celery, finely chopped
- 1½ pounds large raw shrimp, peeled and deveined
- ½ cup all-purpose flour
- 3 eggs
- 3 tablespoons milk
- 2 to 3 cups fresh bread crumbs (8 to 10 bread slices)
- Vegetable oil for frying

*Pick out and discard any shell or cartilage from crabmeat.

1. For sauce, heat 2 tablespoons oil in small saucepan over medium heat. Add onion; cook and stir 3 minutes or until tender. Add curry powder; cook and stir 1 minute. Add 1½ tablespoons wine, satay sauce, 2 teaspoons soy sauce and sugar; cook and stir 2 minutes. Stir in cream; simmer 2 minutes, stirring occasionally. Keep warm.

2. For shrimp, blend egg whites, cornstarch, 1 tablespoon wine and 1 tablespoon soy sauce in medium bowl. Add crabmeat, green onions and celery; mix well.

3. Cut deep slit into, but not through, back of each shrimp.

4. Flatten shrimp slightly. Press crab mixture into slits. Coat each shrimp lightly with flour.

5. Beat eggs and milk with fork in shallow bowl until blended. Place bread crumbs in separate shallow bowl. Place each shrimp, stuffed side up, in egg mixture, spooning egg mixture over shrimp to cover completely. Coat each shrimp with bread crumbs, pressing crumbs lightly onto shrimp. Place shrimp in single layer on baking sheet. Refrigerate 30 minutes.

6. Heat oil in wok or large skillet over high heat to 375°F. Fry shrimp in batches; cook 3 minutes or until golden brown. Drain on paper towels. Serve with sauce.

Makes 4 servings

broiled hunan fish fillets

  3 tablespoons soy sauce
  1 tablespoon finely chopped green onion
  2 teaspoons dark sesame oil
  1 clove garlic, minced
  1 teaspoon minced fresh ginger
  ¼ teaspoon red pepper flakes
  1 pound red snapper, scrod or cod fillets

1. Combine soy sauce, green onion, sesame oil, garlic, ginger and red pepper flakes in small bowl.

2. Spray rack of broiler pan with nonstick cooking spray. Place fish on rack; brush with soy sauce mixture.

3. Broil 4 to 5 inches from heat 10 minutes or until fish begins to flake when tested with fork.

Makes 4 servings

ginger-scented halibut

¼ cup orange juice

2 tablespoons soy sauce

1 ½ teaspoons rice vinegar

½ teaspoon packed brown sugar

1 teaspoon dark sesame oil

4 halibut steaks, about ¾ inch thick

1 tablespoon slivered fresh ginger

Chives or 2 green onions, finely chopped (optional)

1. For sauce, combine orange juice, soy sauce, vinegar and brown sugar in small saucepan; bring to a boil. Remove from heat; stir in sesame oil.

2. Place bamboo steamer or wire steaming rack in wok or large saucepan. Add water to ½ inch below rack. Cover; bring to a boil over high heat. Carefully place halibut on rack in single layer; sprinkle evenly with ginger. Cover; steam 8 to 10 minutes or until halibut begins to flake when tested with fork.

3. Transfer halibut to serving dish. Drizzle with sauce. Garnish with chives.

Makes 4 servings

 Tip Ginger is the root (more accurately, a rhizome) of a tropical plant and is used in a variety of different forms in Asian cooking. The fresh root should be firm and have a smooth skin and a fresh, spicy fragrance. It can be stored at room temperature for up to three weeks. For longer storage, freeze fresh ginger in a sealed bag and thaw slightly to slice off a portion for use.

scallops, shrimp and squid with basil and chiles

½ pound cleaned squid (body tubes, tentacles or a combination)
½ pound sea scallops
¼ cup water
2 tablespoons oyster sauce
1 teaspoon cornstarch
½ to ¾ pound medium raw shrimp, peeled and deveined
1 tablespoon vegetable oil
3 to 4 jalapeño peppers,* thinly sliced
6 cloves garlic, minced
½ cup roasted peanuts
2 green onions, thinly sliced
½ cup slivered fresh basil leaves
Hot cooked rice

Jalapeño peppers can sting and irritate the skin, so wear rubber gloves when handling peppers and do not touch your eyes.

1. Rinse squid; cut body tubes crosswise into ⅓-inch rings. Rinse and drain scallops. Slice large scallops crosswise into halves. Combine water, oyster sauce and cornstarch in small bowl.

2. Fill medium saucepan half full with water; bring to a boil over high heat. Add shrimp; reduce heat to medium. Cook 2 to 3 minutes or until shrimp are pink and opaque. Remove to colander with slotted spoon.

3. Return water to a boil. Add squid; reduce heat to medium. Cook rings 1 minute; cook tentacles 4 minutes. Remove to colander. Return water to a boil. Add scallops; reduce heat to medium. Cook 3 to 4 minutes or until opaque. Remove to colander.

4. Heat oil in wok or large skillet over medium-high heat. Add jalapeño peppers; stir-fry 3 minutes. Add garlic; cook and stir 2 minutes or until garlic is fragrant and peppers are tender.

5. Stir cornstarch mixture; add to wok. Cook and stir until thickened. Add seafood, peanuts and green onions; cook and stir 2 to 3 minutes or until heated through. Stir in basil. Serve with rice. *Makes 4 servings*

shanghai steamed fish

1 cleaned whole sea bass, red snapper or grouper (about 1½ pounds)

¼ cup teriyaki sauce

2 teaspoons grated fresh ginger

2 green onions, cut into 4-inch pieces

Hot cooked rice

1 teaspoon dark sesame oil

Bell pepper strips (optional)

Sliced green onions (optional)

1. Sprinkle inside cavity of fish with teriyaki sauce and ginger. Place green onions in cavity in single layer.

2. Place steaming rack in wok. Add water to ½ inch below rack. Bring to a boil. Reduce heat to medium-low to maintain a simmer. Place fish on steaming rack. Cover and steam fish 10 minutes per inch of thickness measured at thickest part. Fish is done when it begins to flake when tested with fork.

3. Carefully remove fish; discard green onions. Cut fish into 4 portions, removing it from bones. Serve over rice. Sprinkle with sesame oil and garnish with bell pepper strips and sliced green onions, if desired. *Makes 4 servings*

194

garlic prawns with green onion

2 tablespoons cooking oil

1 tablespoon LEE KUM KEE®
Minced Garlic

8 ounces prawns, deveined and
patted dry

2 tablespoons LEE KUM KEE®
Less Sodium Soy Sauce

2 red chile peppers, cut into thin
strips

2 green onions, chopped

1 tablespoon LEE KUM KEE®
Pure Sesame Oil

1. Heat wok or skillet over high heat
until hot. Add cooking oil, LEE KUM
KEE Minced Garlic, prawns and LEE
KUM KEE Less Sodium Soy Sauce; stir-fry
until prawns turn pink.

2. Add chile peppers, green onions and LEE KUM KEE Pure Sesame Oil; cook 1 minute.
Serve immediately.

Makes 2 servings

Prep Time: 15 minutes
Cook Time: 10 minutes

chinese crab cakes

1 pound fresh or pasteurized lump crabmeat* (see Tip)
½ cup plus ⅓ cup panko bread crumbs, divided
2 eggs
2 green onions, finely chopped
1 tablespoon dark sesame oil
1 tablespoon grated fresh ginger
1 tablespoon Chinese hot mustard
2 tablespoons peanut or canola oil, divided
   Prepared sweet and sour sauce

Pick out and discard any shell or cartilage from crabmeat.

1. Combine crabmeat, ½ cup panko, eggs, green onions, sesame oil, ginger and mustard in large bowl; mix well.

2. Shape level ⅓ cupfuls of mixture into 8 patties about ½-inch thick. (At this point, patties may be covered and chilled up to 2 hours.)

3. Heat 1 tablespoon peanut oil in large nonstick skillet over medium heat. Place remaining ⅓ cup panko in shallow dish; dip each crab cake lightly in panko to coat. Add 4 crab cakes to skillet; cook 3 to 4 minutes per side or until golden brown and heated through. (Crab cakes will be soft, so turn them carefully.) Keep warm. Repeat with remaining 1 tablespoon peanut oil and 4 crab cakes. Serve with sweet and sour sauce.

Makes 4 servings

 Tip The different grades and kinds of crabmeat can be confusing, but there are a few main categories that it helps to understand. Fresh crabmeat is from a freshly cooked crab. It is extremely perishable. Crabmeat is more commonly available in pasteurized refrigerated containers from your fishmonger. Once opened the crab in these containers will have a shelf life of about 3 days. There are grades of crab as well. The most expensive is jumbo lump, which can cost $40 a pound. Less costly, but still delicious, are lump, special and claw crabmeat. For crab cakes, one of the less expensive grades is best, since you are adding flavorings and don't need or want large white chunks of crab.

steamed fish over fragrant thai noodles

1 pound thin rice noodles or angel hair pasta
4 cups broccoli, chopped
2 cups assorted sliced mushrooms
2 cups carrots, julienned
1½ cups bean sprouts
1 pound sole fillets
¾ cup unseasoned rice vinegar
½ cup reduced-sodium soy sauce
2 tablespoons minced fresh ginger
1 clove garlic, minced
¼ cup peanut butter
¾ cup thinly sliced green onions
½ cup finely chopped dry-roasted peanuts
¾ cup minced cilantro (optional)

198

Bring 3 quarts water to a boil over high heat. Add the noodles and cook until al dente, about 3 minutes. Drain the noodles and set aside. In a wok or skillet coated with cooking spray, stir-fry the broccoli, mushrooms, carrots and bean sprouts until softened. Toss the noodles and vegetables and set aside. Steam the sole fillets by placing the fillets on a glass plate and cover with plastic wrap or a glass lid. Microwave on high for 3 to 4 minutes. (Or bake the fillets wrapped in foil in a 450°F oven for 4 to 6 minutes.)

To make the dressing, combine the rice vinegar, soy sauce, ginger and garlic in a small bowl. Microwave the peanut butter on high until a liquid-like consistency. Whisk the peanut butter into the dressing. Pour the dressing over the noodles and vegetables and toss well. Arrange the steamed fish fillets on top. Garnish with green onions, peanuts and cilantro.   *Makes 6 servings*

Favorite recipe from **Peanut Advisory Board**

asian honey-tea grilled prawns

1 cup brewed double-strength orange spice tea, cooled
¼ cup honey
¼ cup rice vinegar
¼ cup soy sauce
1 tablespoon finely chopped fresh ginger
½ teaspoon ground black pepper
1½ pounds medium raw shrimp, peeled and deveined
   Salt
2 green onions, thinly sliced

In plastic bag, combine marinade ingredients. Remove ½ cup marinade; set aside for dipping sauce. Add shrimp to marinade in bag, turning to coat. Close bag securely and marinate in refrigerator 30 minutes or up to 12 hours.

Remove shrimp from marinade; discard marinade. Thread shrimp onto 8 skewers, dividing evenly. Grill over medium coals 4 to 6 minutes or until shrimp turn pink and are just firm to the touch, turning once. Season with salt as desired.

Meanwhile, prepare dipping sauce by placing reserved ½ cup marinade in small saucepan. Bring to a boil over medium-high heat. Boil 3 to 5 minutes or until slightly reduced. Stir in green onions. *Makes 4 servings*

Favorite recipe from **National Honey Board**

Chinese New Year

Nobody is better at celebrating with a feast than the Chinese, and New Year is the biggest and most delicious feast of all. Many of these dishes are said to bring good luck and prosperity and they are all a good excuse for a party!

longevity noodle soup

4 teaspoons cornstarch

2 tablespoons water

1 tablespoon sesame oil

8 cups SWANSON® Chicken Broth (Regular, Natural Goodness® or Certified Organic)

3 tablespoons soy sauce

2 eggs, beaten

1 package (1 pound) thin spaghetti, cooked and drained (about 8 cups)

¼ pound sliced cooked ham, cut into 2-inch-long strips (about 1 cup)

4 medium green onions, chopped (about ½ cup)

1. Stir the cornstarch, water and sesame oil in a small bowl until the mixture is smooth.

2. Heat the broth and soy sauce in a 3-quart saucepan over medium heat to a boil. Stir the cornstarch mixture in the saucepan. Cook and stir until the mixture boils and thickens.

3. Reduce the heat to low. Gradually stir the eggs into the saucepan. Remove the saucepan from the heat. Divide the spaghetti, ham and green onions among 8 serving bowls. Spoon about 1 cup broth mixture into each. Serve immediately.

Makes 8 servings

Cook Time: 15 minutes
Prep Time: 20 minutes
Total Time: 35 minutes

clams in black bean sauce

24 small hard-shell clams
1½ tablespoons fermented, salted black beans (see Tip)
2 cloves garlic, minced
1 teaspoon minced fresh ginger
2 tablespoons vegetable oil
2 green onions, thinly sliced
1 cup chicken broth
2 tablespoons rice wine or dry sherry
1 tablespoon soy sauce
1½ to 2 cups thin Chinese wheat noodles (mein), cooked and drained
3 tablespoons chopped fresh cilantro or parsley

1. Scrub clams under cold running water with stiff brush. *Discard any broken shells or those that refuse to close when tapped.*

2. Place black beans in sieve and rinse under cold running water. Coarsely chop beans. Combine beans with garlic and ginger; finely chop all three together.

3. Heat oil in Dutch oven over medium heat. Add black bean mixture and green onions; stir-fry 30 seconds. Add clams and stir to coat.

4. Add broth, wine and soy sauce to Dutch oven. Bring to a boil. Reduce heat; cover and simmer 5 to 8 minutes until clam shells open. *Discard any clams that do not open.*

5. To serve, arrange clams on noodles. Ladle broth over clams. Garnish with cilantro.

Makes 4 servings

 Tip Fermented or salted black beans are black soybeans that have been aged and seasoned to concentrate their flavor. They are available in Asian markets or online. They are the main seasoning in jarred Chinese black bean sauce, which also includes garlic and other flavorings. If you can't find fermented black beans, substitute one or two tablespoons of black bean paste.

baked egg rolls

Sesame Dipping Sauce (page 207)
1 ounce dried shiitake mushrooms
1 large carrot, shredded
1 can (8 ounces) sliced water chestnuts, drained and minced
3 green onions, minced
3 tablespoons chopped fresh cilantro
Nonstick cooking spray
¾ pound ground chicken
2 tablespoons minced fresh ginger
6 cloves garlic, minced
2 tablespoons soy sauce
2 teaspoons water
1 teaspoon cornstarch
12 egg roll wrappers
1 tablespoon vegetable oil
1 teaspoon sesame seeds

1. Prepare Sesame Dipping Sauce; set aside.

2. Place mushrooms in small bowl. Cover with hot water; let stand 30 minutes or until tender. Drain and squeeze out excess water. Cut off and discard stems; finely chop caps. Combine mushrooms, carrot, water chestnuts, green onions and cilantro in large bowl.

3. Spray medium nonstick skillet with cooking spray; heat over medium-high heat. Brown chicken 2 minutes, stirring to break up meat. Drain fat. Add ginger and garlic; cook and stir 2 minutes or until chicken is cooked through. Add to mushroom mixture. Sprinkle with soy sauce; mix thoroughly.

4. Preheat oven to 425°F. Spray baking sheet with cooking spray; set aside.

5. Blend water into cornstarch in small bowl. Lay wrapper on work surface. Spoon about ⅓ cup filling across center of wrapper to within ½ inch of sides. Fold bottom of wrapper over filling. Fold in sides. Brush ½-inch strip across top edge with cornstarch mixture; roll up and seal securely. Place seam side down on baking sheet. Repeat with remaining wrappers, filling and cornstarch mixture.

6. Brush egg rolls with oil. Sprinkle with sesame seeds. Bake 18 minutes or until golden and crisp. Serve with Sesame Dipping Sauce. *Makes 6 servings*

sesame dipping sauce

¼ cup rice vinegar
4 teaspoons soy sauce
2 teaspoons minced fresh ginger
1 teaspoon dark sesame oil

Combine all ingredients in small bowl; blend well. *Makes about ½ cup*

Tip Many dishes and ingredients served for Chinese New Year have symbolic meanings. Egg rolls or spring rolls represent wealth for the coming year. Why? Their shape is said to be similar to a gold bar!

mandarin orange chicken

2 tablespoons rice vinegar

2 tablespoons vegetable oil, divided

2 tablespoons soy sauce

2 teaspoons grated orange peel

1 clove garlic, minced

1 pound boneless skinless chicken breasts, cut into strips

2 cans (11 ounces each) mandarin oranges, undrained

½ cup orange juice

2 tablespoons cornstarch

½ teaspoon red pepper flakes

1 onion, cut into thin wedges

1 small zucchini, sliced

1 red bell pepper, cut into 1-inch pieces

Hot cooked rice

208

1. Combine vinegar, 1 tablespoon oil, soy sauce, orange peel and garlic in medium bowl. Add chicken; toss to coat. Cover and refrigerate 15 minutes to 1 hour.

2. Remove chicken from marinade; reserve marinade. Drain oranges and reserve juice in 2-cup measuring cup; set oranges aside. Add marinade to cup, plus additional orange juice if needed to make 2 cups liquid. Whisk orange juice mixture into cornstarch and red pepper flakes in medium bowl; set aside.

3. Heat remaining 1 tablespoon oil in wok or large skillet over high heat. Add chicken; stir-fry 2 to 3 minutes or until cooked through. Remove chicken.

4. Add onion; stir-fry 1 minute. Add zucchini; stir-fry 1 minute. Add bell pepper; stir-fry 1 minute or until vegetables are crisp-tender. Stir orange juice mixture and add to wok. Cook and stir until mixture comes to a boil; boil 1 minute. Add chicken; cook until heated through. Gently stir in oranges. Serve with rice.   *Makes 6 servings*

scallion pancakes

2¼ cups all-purpose flour, divided
1 teaspoon sugar
⅔ cup boiling water
¼ to ½ cup cold water
2 teaspoons dark sesame oil
½ cup finely chopped green onions
1 teaspoon coarse salt
½ to ¾ cup vegetable oil

1. Combine 2 cups flour and sugar in large bowl. Stir in boiling water and mix just until water is absorbed and mixture forms large clumps. Gradually stir in enough cold water so dough forms a ball and is no longer sticky.

2. Place dough on lightly floured surface; flatten slightly. Knead dough 5 minutes or until smooth and elastic. Wrap dough with plastic wrap; let stand 1 hour.

3. Knead dough briefly on lightly floured surface; divide into 4 pieces. Roll 1 dough piece into 6- to 7-inch round, keeping remaining pieces wrapped in plastic wrap to prevent drying. Brush dough with ½ teaspoon sesame oil; evenly sprinkle with 2 tablespoons green onions and ¼ teaspoon salt. Roll up, jelly-roll style, into tight cylinder.

4. Coil cylinder into a spiral and pinch end under to seal. Repeat with remaining dough pieces, sesame oil, green onions and salt. Cover coiled pieces with plastic wrap and let stand 15 minutes.

5. Roll each coiled piece on lightly floured surface into 6- to 7-inch round with floured rolling pin.

6. Heat ½ cup vegetable oil in wok over medium-high heat until oil registers 375°F. Carefully place pancake into hot oil. Fry 2 to 3 minutes per side or until golden. While pancake is frying, press center lightly with metal spatula to ensure even cooking. Drain on paper towels. Repeat with remaining pancakes, adding vegetable oil if necessary and reheating oil between batches.

7. Cut each pancake into wedges. Serve immediately.

Makes 32 appetizers

stir-fried crab

Sesame Noodle Cake (page 213)

8 ounces firm tofu, drained

1 tablespoon soy sauce

¼ cup chicken broth

3 tablespoons oyster sauce

2 teaspoons cornstarch

1 tablespoon peanut or vegetable oil

2 cups snow peas, cut into halves

½ pound pasteurized lump crabmeat* or imitation crabmeat

2 tablespoons chopped fresh cilantro or thinly sliced green onion

Pick out and discard any shell or cartilage from crabmeat.

1. Prepare Sesame Noodle Cake. Set aside.

2. Press tofu lightly between paper towels; cut into ½-inch squares or triangles. Place in shallow dish. Drizzle soy sauce over tofu.

3. Blend broth and oyster sauce into cornstarch in small bowl until smooth.

4. Heat oil in wok or large skillet over medium-high heat. Add snow peas; stir-fry 2 minutes or until crisp-tender. Add crabmeat; stir-fry 1 minute. Stir broth mixture and add to wok. Cook and stir 30 seconds or until sauce boils and thickens.

5. Stir in tofu mixture; cook and stir until heated through. Serve over Sesame Noodle Cake. Sprinkle with cilantro.   *Makes 4 servings*

Sesame noodle cake

4 ounces uncooked thin Chinese wheat noodles (mein) or vermicelli
1 tablespoon soy sauce
1 tablespoon peanut or vegetable oil
½ teaspoon dark sesame oil

1. Cook noodles according to package directions; drain well. Place in large bowl. Toss with soy sauce.

2. Heat peanut oil in large nonstick skillet over medium heat. Add noodle mixture; pat into even layer with spatula.

3. Cook 6 minutes or until bottom is lightly browned. Invert onto plate, then slide back into skillet, browned side up. Cook 4 minutes or until bottom is browned. Drizzle with sesame oil. Transfer to serving platter and cut into quarters. *Makes 4 servings*

 Tip Noodles are served in many forms for Chinese New Year. They symbolize long life and the longer the noodles the better! Snow peas stand for unity because there are multiple peas in a single pod and they are also said to bring luck for the coming year. So you're sure to enjoy a long, prosperous year after enjoying this dish.

213

spicy new year's wontons

Peanut oil
2 green onions, finely chopped
½ pound ground turkey or chicken
½ cup drained canned black beans
Salsa
1 package wonton wrappers

1. Lightly brush baking sheet with small amount of oil; set aside.

2. Heat 1 tablespoon oil in medium skillet. Add green onions; cook and stir 1 minute. Add turkey; cook 4 to 5 minutes or until no longer pink, stirring to break up meat. Remove skillet from heat. Stir in beans and 7 tablespoons salsa.

3. With point of wonton wrapper facing you, place about 1½ teaspoons turkey mixture in center of wrapper; moisten edges of wrapper with water. Fold wrapper in half to enclose filling. Fold sides of wonton so corners meet. Moisten points with water; press lightly to seal. Place on prepared baking sheet. Repeat with remaining wrappers and turkey mixture.

4. Heat oil in wok or large skillet to 370°F. Fry wontons, a few at a time, 1 to 2 minutes or until golden brown. Drain on paper towels. Serve warm with additional salsa.

Makes about 3 dozen wontons

214

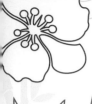

chinatown stuffed mushrooms

24 large mushrooms (about 1 pound)
½ pound ground turkey
1 clove garlic, minced
¼ cup dry bread crumbs
¼ cup thinly sliced green onions
3 tablespoons soy sauce, divided
1 egg white, lightly beaten
1 teaspoon minced fresh ginger
⅛ teaspoon red pepper flakes (optional)

1. Remove stems from mushrooms; finely chop enough stems to equal 1 cup. Cook turkey, chopped stems and garlic in medium skillet over medium-high heat until turkey is no longer pink, stirring to break up meat. Drain fat. Stir in bread crumbs, green onions, 2 tablespoons soy sauce, egg white, ginger and red pepper flakes, if desired; mix well.

2. Preheat broiler. Coat broiler pan with nonstick cooking spray.

3. Brush mushroom caps lightly with remaining 1 tablespoon soy sauce; spoon about 2 teaspoons stuffing into each mushroom cap.* Place stuffed mushrooms on prepared broiler pan. Broil 4 to 5 inches from heat 5 to 6 minutes or until heated through.

Makes 24 appetizers

*Mushrooms can be made ahead to this point; cover and refrigerate up to 24 hours. Add 1 to 2 minutes to broiling time for chilled mushrooms. Or freeze filling in individual portions. To freeze, place portions on cookie sheet or shallow pan; place in freezer 30 minutes to firm slightly. Transfer to freezer food storage bag and freeze completely. Thaw in refrigerator before filling mushrooms as directed.

fan-tailed chinese shrimp

1 tablespoon seasoned rice vinegar
1 tablespoon oyster sauce
1 tablespoon soy sauce
2 cloves garlic, minced
¼ teaspoon red pepper flakes
18 large raw shrimp (about 1 pound),
    peeled and deveined, tails on
1 tablespoon peanut or canola oil
¼ cup chopped fresh cilantro
    Plum sauce or sweet and sour
    sauce (optional)

1. For marinade, combine vinegar, oyster sauce, soy sauce, garlic and red pepper flakes in large bowl; mix well.

2. To butterfly shrimp, use small sharp knife to cut each shrimp down back (where vein was) three fourths of the way through shrimp. Open shrimp; place cut side down on work surface, pressing to flatten into butterfly shape. Add shrimp to bowl with marinade; toss to coat. Cover and refrigerate at least 30 minutes or up to 2 hours.

3. Heat oil in large nonstick skillet over medium heat. Remove shrimp from marinade; discard marinade. Cook shrimp in batches 3 to 4 minutes or until pink and opaque, turning once. Transfer to serving platter; sprinkle with cilantro. Serve with plum sauce for dipping, if desired.

Makes 6 servings

chinese almond cookies

1 package (about 18 ounces) yellow cake mix
5 tablespoons butter, melted
1 egg
1½ teaspoons almond extract
   Whole almonds
1 egg yolk
1 teaspoon water

1. Beat cake mix, butter, egg and almond extract in large bowl with electric mixer at medium speed until well blended. Shape dough into disc; wrap and refrigerate 4 hours or overnight.

2. Preheat oven to 350°F. Spray cookie sheets with nonstick cooking spray.

3. Shape dough into 1-inch balls; place 2 inches apart on prepared cookie sheets. Press almond into center of each ball, flattening slightly.

4. Whisk egg yolk and water in small bowl. Brush tops of cookies with egg yolk mixture. Bake 10 to 12 minutes or until lightly browned. Cool on cookie sheets 5 minutes. Remove to wire racks; cool completely.   *Makes about 2 dozen cookies*

Prep Time: 15 minutes
Chill Time: 4 hours
Bake Time: 10 to 12 minutes

 **Tip** Nobody really knows where the Chinese almond cookie originated. It may have been invented, like chop suey and the fortune cookie, after the first wave of Chinese immigration to the U.S. in the 1800s. Almond cookies are often enjoyed around the New Year and given as gifts.

219

dim sum baked buns

9 frozen bread dough rolls (about 18 ounces)
6 to 8 dried shiitake mushrooms
3 green onions, minced
2 tablespoons plum sauce
1 tablespoon hoisin sauce
Nonstick cooking spray
½ pound ground chicken
4 cloves garlic, minced
1 tablespoon minced fresh ginger
1 egg, beaten
¾ teaspoon sesame seeds

1. Thaw frozen rolls according to package directions.

2. Place mushrooms in small bowl. Cover with hot water; let stand 30 minutes. Drain; squeeze out excess water. Cut off and discard stems. Finely chop caps. Combine mushrooms, green onions, plum sauce and hoisin sauce in large bowl.

3. Spray medium nonstick skillet with cooking spray; heat over high heat. Add chicken; cook 1 to 2 minutes or until no longer pink, stirring to break up meat. Add garlic and ginger; cook and stir 2 minutes. Add mushroom mixture; mix well.

4. Spray two baking sheets with cooking spray. Lightly flour hands and work surface. Cut each roll in half; roll each piece into a ball. Shape each piece into 3- to 3½-inch disc. Press edges of discs to flatten. (Centers of discs should be thicker than edges.)

5. Place generous tablespoon filling in centers of discs. Lift edges of dough up and around filling; pinch to seal. Place seam sides down on baking sheet.

6. Cover buns with towel; let rise in warm place 45 minutes or until buns have doubled in size.

7. Meanwhile, preheat oven to 375°F. Brush buns with egg, then sprinkle with sesame seeds. Bake 16 to 18 minutes or until buns are golden brown. *Makes 18 buns*

braised lion's head

Meatballs

- 1 pound ground pork
- ¼ pound raw shrimp, peeled and finely chopped
- ¼ cup sliced water chestnuts, finely chopped
- 1 egg, lightly beaten
- 1 green onion, finely chopped
- 1 tablespoon cornstarch
- 1 tablespoon rice wine or dry sherry
- 1 tablespoon soy sauce
- 1 teaspoon minced fresh ginger
- ½ teaspoon salt
- ½ teaspoon sugar
- 2 tablespoons vegetable oil

Sauce

- 1½ cups chicken broth
- 2 tablespoons soy sauce
- ½ teaspoon sugar
- 1 head napa cabbage (1½ to 2 pounds), cut into large pieces
- 2 tablespoons cornstarch
- 3 tablespoons water
- 1 teaspoon dark sesame oil

1. Combine all meatball ingredients except vegetable oil in large bowl; mix well. Shape mixture into 8 balls. Heat vegetable oil in wok or large skillet over medium-high heat. Add meatballs; cook 6 to 8 minutes or until browned, stirring occasionally.

2. Transfer meatballs to large saucepan; discard drippings. Add broth, 2 tablespoons soy sauce and ½ teaspoon sugar. Bring to a boil. Reduce heat to low; cover. Simmer 30 minutes. Place cabbage over meatballs; cover. Simmer 10 minutes.

3. Transfer cabbage and meatballs to serving platter. Blend 2 tablespoons cornstarch and water in small bowl. Gradually add to pan juices; cook until slightly thickened, stirring constantly. Stir in sesame oil. Serve over meatballs and cabbage.

Makes 4 to 6 servings

shrimp toast

12 large raw shrimp, peeled and deveined, tails on
 1 egg
 2 tablespoons plus 1½ teaspoons cornstarch
¼ teaspoon salt
   Black pepper
 3 slices white sandwich bread, cut into 4 triangles
 1 hard-cooked egg yolk, cut into ½-inch pieces
 1 slice (1 ounce) cooked ham, cut into ½-inch pieces
 1 green onion, finely chopped
   Vegetable oil for frying

1. Cut deep slit down back of each shrimp; press gently with fingers to flatten.

2. Beat egg, cornstarch, salt and pepper in large bowl until blended. Add shrimp; toss to coat.

3. Drain each shrimp and press, cut side down, onto each piece of bread. Brush small amount of remaining egg mixture onto each shrimp.

4. Place piece of hard-cooked egg yolk and ham and pinch of green onion on top of each shrimp.

5. Heat 1 inch oil in wok or large skillet over medium-high heat to 375°F. Add three or four bread pieces at a time; cook 1 to 2 minutes, then spoon hot oil over shrimp until cooked through and toast is golden brown. Drain on paper towels.

Makes 12 appetizers

pineapple-hoisin hens

2 cloves garlic
1 can (8 ounces) crushed pineapple in juice, undrained
2 tablespoons rice vinegar
2 tablespoons soy sauce
2 tablespoons hoisin sauce
2 teaspoons minced fresh ginger
1 teaspoon Chinese five-spice powder*
2 large Cornish hens (about 1½ pounds each), split in half

Chinese five-spice powder consists of cinnamon, cloves, fennel seed, star anise and Szechuan peppercorns.

1. Mince garlic in blender or food processor. Add pineapple with juice; process until fairly smooth. Add vinegar, soy sauce, hoisin sauce, ginger and five-spice powder; process 5 seconds.

2. Place hens in large resealable food storage bag; pour pineapple mixture over hens. Seal bag; turn to coat. Marinate in refrigerator at least 2 hours or up to 24 hours, turning once.

3. Preheat oven to 375°F. Remove hens from marinade; reserve marinade. Place hens, skin side up, on rack in shallow, foil-lined roasting pan. Roast 35 minutes.

4. Brush hens lightly with reserved marinade; discard remaining marinade. Roast 10 minutes or until hens are browned and cooked through (165°F).

Makes 4 servings

Tip Pineapple is another ingredient often included in recipes for Chinese New Year. It represents wealth, luck (including gambling luck) and good fortune.

Asian–American

One of the best things about living in a country that is a melting pot is the food! Asian immigrants created many of our favorite dishes, including chop suey, fortune cookies and California Roll Sushi. Isn't diversity delicious?

apricot beef with sesame noodles

1 beef top sirloin steak (about 1 pound)

3 tablespoons Dijon mustard

3 tablespoons soy sauce

2 packages (3 ounces each) uncooked ramen noodles, any flavor*

2 tablespoons vegetable oil

2 cups (6 ounces) snow peas

1 medium red bell pepper, cut into cubes

¾ cup apricot preserves

½ cup beef broth

3 tablespoons chopped green onions

2 tablespoons sesame seeds, toasted,** divided

Discard seasoning packet.

**To toast sesame seeds, spread in small skillet. Shake skillet over medium-low heat about 3 minutes or until seeds begin to pop and turn golden.

1. Cut beef lengthwise in half, then crosswise into ¼-inch strips. Combine beef, mustard and soy sauce in medium resealable food storage bag. Seal bag; shake to coat. Marinate in refrigerator 4 hours or overnight.

2. Cook noodles according to package directions. Drain.

3. Heat oil in large skillet over medium-high heat. Add half of beef with marinade; stir-fry 2 minutes. Remove to bowl. Repeat with remaining beef and marinade. Return beef to skillet. Add snow peas and bell pepper; stir-fry 2 minutes. Add noodles, preserves, broth, green onions and 1 tablespoon sesame seeds. Cook 1 minute or until heated through. Top with remaining sesame seeds. *Makes 4 to 6 servings*

thai-style pork chops with cucumber sauce

3 tablespoons Thai peanut sauce, divided
¼ teaspoon red pepper flakes
4 bone-in pork chops (5 ounces each)
1 container (6 ounces) plain yogurt
¼ cup diced cucumber
2 tablespoons chopped red onion
2 tablespoons finely chopped fresh mint or cilantro
1 teaspoon sugar

1. Prepare grill for direct cooking or preheat broiler. Combine 2 tablespoons peanut sauce and red pepper flakes in small bowl; brush evenly over both sides of pork chops. Let stand while preparing cucumber sauce or refrigerate up to 4 hours.

2. Combine yogurt, cucumber, onion, mint and sugar in medium bowl; mix well. Grill chops, covered, over medium heat or broil 4 inches from heat source 4 minutes; turn and cook 3 minutes or until barely pink in center. Just before removing from heat, baste with remaining 1 tablespoon peanut sauce. Serve chops with cucumber sauce.

Makes 4 servings

 Tip Purchase prepared peanut sauce or make your own if you like. A simple recipe is on page 72 with the recipe for Tofu Satay. A typical recipe includes peanut butter, coconut milk, garlic and spices. Leftover peanut sauce is delicious on noodles or as a dipping sauce for satay.

fortune cookies

Nonstick cooking spray
2 egg whites
⅓ cup all-purpose flour
⅓ cup sugar
1 tablespoon water
¼ teaspoon vanilla
12 paper fortunes*

Write your own fortunes on small strips of paper.

1. Preheat oven to 400°F. Spray cookie sheets with cooking spray.

2. Whisk egg whites in small bowl until foamy. Add flour, sugar, water and vanilla; whisk until smooth.

3. Working in batches of 2, place 2 teaspoons batter on prepared cookie sheet for each cookie. Spread batter evenly with back of spoon to 3-inch round. Spray with cooking spray. Bake 4 minutes or until edges are golden brown.

4. Working quickly, remove cookies from cookie sheet and invert onto work surface. Place fortune in centers. Fold cookies in half, pressing on seam. Fold in half again, pressing to hold together. Cool completely. Repeat steps 3 and 4 with remaining batter and fortunes.

Makes 1 dozen cookies

Tip There are no fortune cookies in China. This classic cookie served at every Chinese restaurant is an American invention that probably came from Asian immigrants living in California around the turn of the century. Making your own fortune cookies allows you to decide the future!

sesame hoisin beer-can chicken

1 can (12 ounces) beer, divided
½ cup hoisin sauce
2 tablespoons honey
1 tablespoon soy sauce
1 teaspoon chili garlic sauce
½ teaspoon dark sesame oil
1 whole chicken (3½ to 4 pounds)

1. Prepare grill for indirect cooking.

2. Combine 2 tablespoons beer, hoisin sauce, honey, soy sauce, chili garlic sauce and sesame oil in small bowl. Gently loosen skin of chicken over breast meat, legs and thighs. Spoon half of hoisin mixture under skin. Reserve remaining hoisin mixture.

3. Pour off beer until can is two-thirds full. Hold chicken upright with opening of cavity pointing down. Insert beer can into cavity. Stand chicken upright on can over drip pan. Spread legs slightly to help support chicken. Grill, covered, 30 minutes over medium heat.

4. Brush chicken with remaining hoisin mixture. Grill, covered, 45 to 60 minutes or until chicken is cooked through (165°F). Use metal tongs to transfer chicken to cutting board; let rest, standing up, 5 minutes. Carefully remove beer can and discard. Carve chicken and serve.

Makes 8 to 10 servings

fried rice with ham

2 tablespoons vegetable oil, divided
2 eggs, beaten
1 small onion, chopped
1 carrot, chopped
⅔ cup diced ham
½ cup frozen green peas
1 clove garlic, minced
3 cups cold cooked rice
3 tablespoons soy sauce
⅛ teaspoon black pepper

1. Heat 1 tablespoon oil in wok or large skillet over medium-high heat. Add eggs; rotate skillet to swirl eggs into thin layer. Cook until set and slightly brown; break up with wooden spoon. Remove from skillet to small bowl.

2. Heat remaining 1 tablespoon oil. Add onion and carrot; stir-fry 2 minutes. Add ham, peas and garlic; stir-fry 1 minute.

3. Add rice; stir-fry 2 to 3 minutes or until rice is heated through. Stir in soy sauce and pepper until well blended. Stir in cooked eggs.   *Makes 4 servings*

Variation: Substitute leftover cooked vegetables for the carrots and peas in this recipe.

grilled chinese salmon

3 tablespoons soy sauce

2 tablespoons rice wine or dry sherry

2 cloves garlic, minced

4 salmon fillets or steaks (about 1 pound)

2 tablespoons finely chopped fresh cilantro

1. Combine soy sauce, wine and garlic in shallow dish. Add salmon; turn to coat. Cover; marinate in refrigerator at least 30 minutes or up to 2 hours.

2. Prepare grill for direct cooking. Remove salmon from marinade; reserve marinade. Place salmon on oiled grid over medium-high heat. Grill 10 minutes or until center is opaque. Baste with reserved marinade after 5 minutes of cooking; discard any remaining marinade. Sprinkle with cilantro. *Makes 4 servings*

peanut-sauced pasta

⅓ cup vegetable broth

3 tablespoons creamy peanut butter

2 tablespoons seasoned rice vinegar

2 tablespoons soy sauce

½ teaspoon red pepper flakes

9 ounces uncooked multigrain linguine

1½ pounds fresh asparagus, cut into 1-inch pieces

⅓ cup unsalted roasted peanuts, chopped

1. Heat broth, peanut butter, vinegar, soy sauce and red pepper flakes in small saucepan over low heat, stirring frequently. Keep warm.

2. Cook pasta according to package directions. Add asparagus for last 5 minutes of cooking. Drain. Toss with peanut sauce. Sprinkle with peanuts. *Makes 6 servings*

korean soft tacos

¼ cup granulated sugar

¼ cup rice wine vinegar

2 tablespoons soy sauce

1 ORTEGA® Soft Taco Kit—includes 10 flour soft tortillas, 1 packet
    (1.25 ounces) taco seasoning mix and 1 packet (3 ounces) taco sauce

2 pounds thin-sliced rib-eye steaks

2 cups bean sprouts

1 red bell pepper, cut into strips

1 yellow bell pepper, cut into strips

6 green onions, diced

2 tablespoons sesame oil

2 limes, cut into wedges

Combine sugar, vinegar, soy sauce and taco sauce from Taco Kit in medium bowl. Add steaks; toss gently to coat with marinade. Cover; marinate in refrigerator 2 hours.

Combine bean sprouts, bell peppers and green onions in medium bowl. Sprinkle with seasoning mix from Taco Kit; toss gently. Set aside.

Remove steaks from marinade; slice into long strips. Reserve any marinade.

Heat sesame oil in large skillet over medium heat. Add steak strips and sear lightly. Add 2 to 3 tablespoons remaining marinade mixture; cook and stir 3 to 4 minutes or until steak is cooked to desired doneness. Discard remaining marinade.

Wrap tortillas from Taco Kit with a clean, lightly moistened cloth or paper towels. Microwave on HIGH (100% power) 1 minute or until hot and pliable.

Divide beef mixture evenly among tortillas. Garnish with taco-seasoned vegetables. Serve with lime wedges.

Makes 10 tacos

Prep Time: 10 minutes
Start to Finish: 2 hours 20 minutes

thai pizza

1 package JENNIE-O TURKEY STORE® Breast Strips
2 teaspoons bottled or fresh minced ginger
2 teaspoons bottled or fresh minced garlic
¼ teaspoon crushed red pepper flakes
  Cooking spray
¼ cup hoisin or stir-fry sauce
1 large (12-inch) prepared pizza crust
⅓ cup thinly sliced green onions
½ teaspoon finely grated lime peel
⅓ cup coarsely chopped roasted peanuts
2 tablespoons chopped cilantro or basil

Heat oven to 450°F. Toss turkey strips with ginger, garlic and pepper flakes. Coat large nonstick skillet with cooking spray; heat over medium-high heat. Add turkey; stir-fry 2 minutes. Add hoisin sauce; stir-fry 2 minutes. Place pizza crust on large cookie sheet. Spread mixture evenly over pizza crust; sprinkle with green onions and lime peel. Bake 8 to 10 minutes or until crust is golden brown and hot. Sprinkle with peanuts and cilantro. Cut into wedges.   *Makes 6 main-dish or 12 appetizer servings*

Prep Time: 15 minutes
Cook Time: 15 minutes

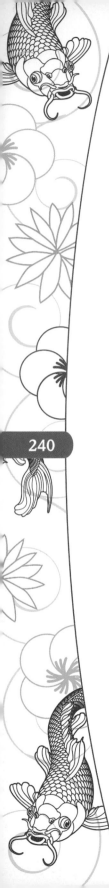

oriental salsa

1 cup diced cucumber
½ cup thinly sliced green onions
½ cup chopped red bell pepper
⅓ cup coarsely chopped fresh cilantro
2 tablespoons soy sauce
1 tablespoon rice vinegar
1 clove garlic, minced
½ teaspoon dark sesame oil
¼ teaspoon red pepper flakes
   Easy Wonton Chips (recipe follows) or assorted fresh vegetables for dipping

1. Combine cucumber, green onions, bell pepper, cilantro, soy sauce, vinegar, garlic, sesame oil and red pepper flakes in medium bowl until well blended.

2. Cover and refrigerate until serving time. Serve with Easy Wonton Chips or assorted fresh vegetables for dipping. Or use as an accompaniment to broiled fish, chicken or pork.

Makes 4 servings

easy wonton chips

1 tablespoon soy sauce
2 teaspoons peanut or vegetable oil
½ teaspoon sugar
¼ teaspoon garlic salt
12 wonton wrappers
   Nonstick cooking spray

1. Preheat oven to 375°F. Combine soy sauce, oil, sugar and garlic salt in small bowl; mix well.

2. Cut each wonton wrapper diagonally in half. Place on baking pan coated with cooking spray. Brush soy sauce mixture lightly over both sides of wrappers.

3. Bake 4 to 6 minutes or until crisp and lightly browned, turning after 3 minutes. Transfer to wire rack; cool completely.

Makes 2 dozen chips

beef and asparagus stir-fry

¾ cup water

3 tablespoons soy sauce

3 tablespoons hoisin sauce

1 tablespoon cornstarch

1 tablespoon peanut or vegetable oil

1 pound beef sirloin, cut into thin strips

1 teaspoon dark sesame oil

8 shiitake mushrooms, stems removed and caps thinly sliced

1 cup baby corn

8 ounces asparagus (8 to 10 medium spears), cut into 1-inch pieces

1 cup snow peas

½ cup red bell pepper strips

½ cup cherry tomato halves

Hot cooked rice (optional)

1. Whisk water, soy sauce, hoisin sauce and cornstarch in small bowl; set aside.

2. Heat peanut oil in wok or large skillet over medium-high heat. Add beef; cook and stir 5 to 6 minutes or until still slightly pink. Remove beef to plate with slotted spoon.

3. Add sesame oil, mushrooms and baby corn to wok; cook and stir 2 to 3 minutes or until mushrooms are tender and corn is heated through. Add asparagus, snow peas and bell pepper; cook and stir 1 minute or until vegetables are crisp-tender.

4. Return beef and any accumulated juices to skillet. Stir reserved soy sauce mixture and add to skillet with tomatoes. Cook and stir 1 minute or until heated through and sauce is thickened. Serve with rice, if desired. *Makes 4 servings*

241

california roll sushi

Sushi Rice (recipe follows)
3 sheets toasted nori
9 tablespoons crabmeat or imitation crabmeat
6 baby carrots, cut into matchstick-size pieces
1 avocado, cut into thin lengthwise slices
Soy sauce, prepared wasabi and pickled ginger (optional)

1. Prepare Sushi Rice. Keep covered at room temperature.

2. Prepare small bowl with water and splash of rice vinegar to rinse fingers and prevent rice from sticking to hands while working. Place sheet of nori, shiny side down, on bamboo rolling mat (lined with plastic wrap, if desired) with wide side of nori aligned with edge closest to you. Wet fingers and spread about 1 cup rice over nori. Leave ½-inch border at top edge of nori to seal roll.

3. Arrange 3 tablespoons crabmeat crosswise on rice about 1½ inches from bottom of nori. Place several carrot pieces over crabmeat. Place 2 or 3 avocado slices next to carrots.

4. Working from bottom, firmly roll up nori sheet into 8-inch log. Press gently to compact rice and keep fillings centered. Press log gently to seal and place seam side down on cutting board. Repeat with remaining nori and fillings.

5. Cut each roll into 6 pieces using sharp knife; wipe knife with wet cloth between cuts to slice cleanly. Serve with soy sauce, wasabi and pickled ginger, if desired.

Makes 3 rolls

Sushi Rice: Bring 1¾ cups water to a boil in medium saucepan. Add ½ teaspoon salt. Stir in 1 cup short grain sushi rice; reduce heat to low. Simmer, covered, 20 minutes or until water is absorbed. Remove from heat; let stand 5 minutes. Transfer to shallow bowl; let cool slightly. Sprinkle with ⅓ cup seasoned rice vinegar and stir gently.

ginger-teriyaki salad with fried chicken tenders

1 package (about 12 ounces) cooked breaded chicken tenders
¼ cup teriyaki sauce
3 tablespoons sugar
3 tablespoons cider vinegar
2 tablespoons dark sesame oil
1½ teaspoons minced fresh ginger
⅛ teaspoon red pepper flakes
1 bag (5 ounces) spring greens mix
1 cup broccoli florets
1 cup shredded carrots
½ cup chopped green onions
¼ cup peanuts, toasted*

To toast peanuts, spread in single layer in small skillet. Cook and stir over medium heat 3 minutes or until fragrant and beginning to brown. Immediately remove from skillet.

244

1. Heat chicken tenders according to package directions. Cut into ½-inch pieces.

2. Combine teriyaki sauce, sugar, vinegar, sesame oil, ginger, and red pepper flakes in small jar with tight-fitting lid. Cover and shake until well blended.

3. Combine spring greens mix, broccoli, carrots and green onions in large bowl. Add teriyaki mixture and toss to coat completely. Top with equal amounts chicken and peanuts.

Makes 4 servings

asian glazed short ribs

4 pounds beef short ribs
1 envelope LIPTON® RECIPE SECRETS® Onion Soup Mix
½ cup apricot preserves
½ cup chili sauce
¼ cup firmly packed light brown sugar
¼ cup soy sauce
2 tablespoons apple cider vinegar
1 tablespoon cornstarch
1 cup water

Slow Cooker Directions

1. In slow cooker, arrange ribs. Combine LIPTON® RECIPE SECRETS® Onion Soup Mix with remaining ingredients, except cornstarch and water.

2. Cook, covered, on LOW 8 to 10 hours or on HIGH 4 to 6 hours, or until ribs are tender.

3. Remove ribs to serving platter; keep warm. In small bowl, combine cornstarch with water. Stir into sauce and cook, covered, 10 to 15 minutes or until thickened. Pour sauce over ribs.

Makes 4 servings

chicken chop suey

1 package (1 ounce) dried shiitake mushrooms
3 tablespoons soy sauce
1 tablespoon cornstarch
1 pound boneless skinless chicken breasts or thighs
2 cloves garlic, minced
1 tablespoon peanut or vegetable oil
½ cup thinly sliced celery
½ cup sliced water chestnuts
½ cup sliced bamboo shoots
1 cup reduced-sodium chicken broth
2 cups hot cooked white rice or chow mein noodles
   Thinly sliced green onions (optional)

1. Place mushrooms in small bowl; cover with hot water. Soak 30 minutes. Drain; squeeze out excess water. Discard stems. Cut caps into quarters.

2. Blend soy sauce with cornstarch in cup until smooth.

3. Cut chicken into 1-inch pieces; toss with garlic in small bowl. Heat oil in wok or large skillet over medium-high heat. Add chicken mixture and celery; stir-fry 2 minutes. Add water chestnuts and bamboo shoots; stir-fry 1 minute. Add broth and mushrooms; cook and stir 3 minutes or until chicken is cooked through.

4. Stir soy sauce mixture and add to wok. Cook and stir 1 to 2 minutes or until sauce boils and thickens. Serve over rice. Garnish with green onions.   *Makes 4 servings*

Acknowledgments

The publisher would like to thank the companies and organizations listed below
for the use of their recipes and photographs in this publication.

Campbell Soup Company

Equal® sweetener

Jennie-O Turkey Store, LLC

Lee Kum Kee®

National Honey Board

Ortega®, A Division of B&G Foods, Inc.

Peanut Advisory Board

Reckitt Benckiser LLC.

Riviana Foods Inc.

Unilever

255

METRIC CONVERSION CHART

VOLUME MEASUREMENTS (dry)

$^1/_8$ teaspoon = 0.5 mL
$^1/_4$ teaspoon = 1 mL
$^1/_2$ teaspoon = 2 mL
$^3/_4$ teaspoon = 4 mL
1 teaspoon = 5 mL
1 tablespoon = 15 mL
2 tablespoons = 30 mL
$^1/_4$ cup = 60 mL
$^1/_3$ cup = 75 mL
$^1/_2$ cup = 125 mL
$^2/_3$ cup = 150 mL
$^3/_4$ cup = 175 mL
1 cup = 250 mL
2 cups = 1 pint = 500 mL
3 cups = 750 mL
4 cups = 1 quart = 1 L

VOLUME MEASUREMENTS (fluid)

1 fluid ounce (2 tablespoons) = 30 mL
4 fluid ounces ($^1/_2$ cup) = 125 mL
8 fluid ounces (1 cup) = 250 mL
12 fluid ounces (1$^1/_2$ cups) = 375 mL
16 fluid ounces (2 cups) = 500 mL

WEIGHTS (mass)

$^1/_2$ ounce = 15 g
1 ounce = 30 g
3 ounces = 90 g
4 ounces = 120 g
8 ounces = 225 g
10 ounces = 285 g
12 ounces = 360 g
16 ounces = 1 pound = 450 g

DIMENSIONS

$^1/_{16}$ inch = 2 mm
$^1/_8$ inch = 3 mm
$^1/_4$ inch = 6 mm
$^1/_2$ inch = 1.5 cm
$^3/_4$ inch = 2 cm
1 inch = 2.5 cm

OVEN TEMPERATURES

250°F = 120°C
275°F = 140°C
300°F = 150°C
325°F = 160°C
350°F = 180°C
375°F = 190°C
400°F = 200°C
425°F = 220°C
450°F = 230°C

BAKING PAN SIZES

Utensil	Size in Inches/Quarts	Metric Volume	Size in Centimeters
Baking or Cake Pan (square or rectangular)	8×8×2	2 L	20×20×5
	9×9×2	2.5 L	23×23×5
	12×8×2	3 L	30×20×5
	13×9×2	3.5 L	33×23×5
Loaf Pan	8×4×3	1.5 L	20×10×7
	9×5×3	2 L	23×13×7
Round Layer Cake Pan	8×1½	1.2 L	20×4
	9×1½	1.5 L	23×4
Pie Plate	8×1¼	750 mL	20×3
	9×1¼	1 L	23×3
Baking Dish or Casserole	1 quart	1 L	—
	1½ quart	1.5 L	—
	2 quart	2 L	—